Exploring the Neighborhood Pronghorn Community

Exploring the Neighborhood Pronghorn Community

Pronghorn Antelope Observation and Zooarchaeology in Colorado

James J. Szczur

Photography by James J. Szczur, Jasmine A. Szczur, and others as noted.

Professor Jim Publishing

Contents

* * *

EXPLORING THE NEIGHBORHOOD PRONGHORN COMMUNITY

Second Edition

Pronghorn Antelope Observation and Zooarchaeology in Colorado

JAMES J. SZCZUR

Professor Jim Publishing

NEW YORK LONDON TORONTO SYDNEY NEW DELHI

The pronghorn herd next door.

No two pronghorn horns are the same.

Book Info & Credits

Professor Jim Publishing
P.O. Box 63104
Colorado Springs, Colorado 80962

For information about special discounts for bulk purchases, please contact Special Sales at above address or by email: *James.Szczur07@gmail.com*
We support bringing Authors to your live event. For more information or to book an event, contact Speakers Bureau at above address or by email: *James.Szczur07@gmail.com*

Exploring the Neighborhood Pronghorn Community (second edition), 9x6 B&W format, by James J. Szczur
ISBN: 978-1-0881-9039-5

Author website: *https://JamesSzczur.wordpress.com/*

Cover, interior design, and photographs (except as cited) by J. Szczur

PHOTO AND ILLUSTRATION CREDITS

Photos, figures, and illustrations are original by the author, unless cited below:
Fig. 1a, top petroglyph photo from World Atlas (https://www.worldatlas.com/articles/what-is-a-petroglyph.html) by author Sharon Omondi
Fig. 1b, bottom petroglyph photo (https://www.pinterest.com/pin/330029478913196370/) by author Lola Stude
Fig. 3, screenshot map from Google.com by author James Szczur
Fig. 7, Montana Outdoors27by author Angela Montana
Fig. 8a, top, Thompson (https://www.freepik.com/photos/antelope) antelope photo created by author by rdyak
Fig. 8b, left, Northern Desert Photography blog by permission, (https://northerndesert.files.wordpress.com/2021/09/mg_5899.jpg?w=2048) by author Alison Hardenburgh
Fig. 8c, right, Unsplash (https://unsplash.com/photos/bsfXvI25iNg) by author Charl Durand
Fig. 9, Northern Desert Photography blog by permission, (https://northerndesertphotography.com/2021/09/12/pronghorn/) by author Alison Hardenburgh
Fig. 10, Pronghorn Phylogeny29aby author Gretchen Newberry and 21.
Kmcandre21 (originally from Price, Bininda-Emonds, and Gittleman, 2005) http://www.ultimateungulate.com/Artiodactyla.html
Fig. 11, Darren Naish, Tetrapod38
Fig. 12, Benji Paysnoe, National Park Service, Tule32
Fig. 13, Charles Alsheimer, Realtree1
Fig. 14, Ajah Lagos (animal-horns-2739117)21aalso at https://www.atlanticcoralenterprise.com/ProductCart/pc/viewCategories.asp?id-

Category=457)
Fig. 15, Brian K. Hall16Based on data in O'Gara and Matson (1975) (O'Gara BW, Matson G. 1975. Growth and casting of horns by pronghorns and exfoliation of horns by bovids.Journal of Mammalogy 56: 829–846)
Fig. 22, Brent Huffman18
Fig. 23, Wyoming Department of Transportation (https://www.conteches.com/knowledge-center/case-studies/details/slug/wydot-highway-191 — -trappers-point)
Fig. 25, Go Hunt14, photo credit: Earthisland.org
Fig. 26. Colorado Parks and Wildlife37
Fig. 27a, left, The Nature Conservancy11
Fig. 27b, right Donald M. Jones.com Montana Fish, Wildlife and Parks25
Fig. 28, Montana Fish, Wildlife and Parks25
Fig. 32a, top, Dreamstime (https://www.stockfreeimages.com/14855362/Pronghorn-Doe-and-Fawn.html) ID: 14855362 by author Jmt0826
Fig. 32b, bottom, Unsplash (https://unsplash.com/photos/ImIFv9oYsYg) by author Emmanuel Boussuge @pluffy98
Fig. 37, Jackrabbit blog (https://a-z-animals.com/blog/what-do-jackrabbits-eat/) by Taiwo Victor
Fig. 41, Jessica20
Fig. 49, James Yule43
Fig. 50, Northern Desert Photography blog by permission, (https://northerndesert.files.wordpress.com/2021/09/mg_9761.jpg?w=2048) by author Alison Hardenburgh

Dedication

This book is dedicated to my lovely wife, LaDonna, who has shared this adventure and so much more.

To my children, who also have learned more about pronghorn than they ever imagined.

To my parents, who have been waiting patiently to read this literary work.

Professor Jim

About the Author

Award winning author, James J. Szczur (Professor Jim), is a zooarchaeological researcher, wildlife photographer, engineer, and university professor. His book, *Exploring the Neighborhood Pronghorn Community, second edition,* won the prestigious "Pages & Paws 7 Most SURPRISING Reads of 2022" award. Living in Colorado, he grew up near Philadelphia PA. A scientist at heart, he is always looking for his next adventure!

Throughout his adventures, Professor Jim has traveled to 39 of the 50 United States and to 25 foreign countries from South America and Europe to the outer reaches of Australia and the Middle East. Out of the 29 U.S. National Parks (NP) he has visited, his favorites are Petrified Forrest NP Arizona (home of Newspaper Rock), Arches NP Utah, Petroglyphs NP New Mexico, and Dinosaur NP Colorado (amazing dinosaur artifacts), each a national treasure preserving ancient Native American and wildlife artifacts. A particularly favorite wildlife safari was wallaby and kangaroo encounters in viper-infested central Australia in 2012.

Now, Professor Jim springs into action to take advantage of a fleeting opportunity to research pronghorn in his own Colorado Springs neighborhood. He perfects a blend of science and adventure while richly illustrating this literary treasure. He shares with the reader his cognitive, emotional, and spiritual impressions encountered during this "not so far from home" wilderness pronghorn expedition.

Foreword

Kristine Lowder

Loved It! This nimble read is a skillful, engaging blend of science, adventure, and inspiration. Fascinating, informative, and compelling!

How did pronghorn antelope become iconic symbols of the American West? Why is the term "antelope" more common than "pronghorn"? What is the pronghorn's closest relative based on DNA? What is the fastest land animal in the world outside of the African cheetah?

Dive into this fascinating and nimble read for answers to all of this and more with *Exploring the Neighborhood Pronghorn Community.* This non-fiction work is a skillful blend of science and adventure. Written in a lively and upbeat style, the author chronicles his "cognitive, emotional, and spiritual impressions" during eighteen months of "pronghorn safaris" in the wilds of Colorado. His intent is to present research, observations, and discoveries of a pronghorn herd to satisfy his long-held curiosity about pronghorn life.

And he delivers. In spades.

If you're thinking this is a dull scientific text or a book on animal husbandry that's as dull as a blunt spoon, fear not! Because this is none of the above. It's an informative and immensely engaging "up close and personal" look at these amazing "high plains drifters" on hooves. It shows readers how fearless and curious pronghorn are. What incredibly keen eyesight, hearing, and smell they have and the beauty, grace, and timelessness of their wilderness environment.

The author skillfully interweaves his own story and experiences into the narrative along with his wilderness adventures. While watching the fleet-footed pronghorn, for example, he often ruminates about the brevity of life and the passage of time.

Just shy of one hundred pages, Pronghorn is chockful of interesting details about the history, habitat, body structure, and behavior of these beautiful creatures. The text is richly illustrated with color photos. These enhance the reader's understanding of these magnificent animals. Aerial maps, charts, and figures are also included in this compelling and absorbing read.

Chapters are well-organized and cogent. They feature a variety of information and observations related to pronghorn life. These include pronghorn social structure and behavior, the etymology of the word "pronghorn," herd communication, and preservation efforts. The text is thoughtful and measured, with an excellent eye for detail. I learned a lot about these beautiful, fleet animals.

The author, also known as "Professor Jim," is an adjunct professor of engineering, freelance wildlife researcher, and photographer. His adventures and insights related to pronghorn antelope make for a rich and fascinating read. In fact, the author's passion for these majestic animals shines through in every page. It's easy to get lost in this enriching, incandescent read. And never want to come back.

I'm glad I grabbed this book. You will be, too!

– Kristine Lowder, Reedsy Reviewer

Call of the pronghorn.

Acknowledgments

A sincere thank you to all those who have contributed to bringing this book a reality. Specific words of thanks follow.

Thank You to the publishing team of the first edition who helped create the foundational material used in this second edition.

Thank You to the photographers who have provided privately owned photographs as well as "public domain stock photos" used in this work to better describe my observations and promote the progress of science and useful arts.

Above all, I thank God for all of His blessings and the ability and passion to explore His world and inspire me to write this book. I am grateful to have been able to follow my curiosity, immerse myself into His creation, and share what I have experienced in this literary work.

Every good gift and every perfect gift is from above,
coming down from the Father. **James 1:17**

For everything created by God is good, and nothing is to be rejected
if it is received with thanksgiving. **1 Timothy 4:4**

Get outdoors and enjoy the beauty and wonder of His creation!

– Professor Jim

Preface

This Second Edition of *Exploring the Neighborhood Pronghorn Community* provides additional photographs and editorial updates. Photographs were added to enhance "interior design" of the book. For example, photographs were added before a new section or chapter to set the stage for the new topic. These photos usually have a caption with no assigned figure number. Some figures have a "part 2" or "part 3" to allow multi-photograph pictures to be enlarged over more than one page. Additionally, the improved book design features a 7x10-inch book size. A more economical 9x6 black and white print format was created to provide a super-low print price option. In all, these improvements aim to greatly enhance the reader experience.

The original purpose of this literary work was to present research observations and discoveries of a pronghorn herd located near my home in Colorado Springs. These "pronghorn safaris" occurred from November 2020 through May 2022 involving 53 trips and over 320 hours in the field. My pronghorn safaris involved observation, picture taking, and artifact collecting. No hunting or injury to wildlife occurred at any time.

Entering Colorado pronghorn territory to observe their habits and behavior was a new adventure for me, and satisfied my long-held curiosity about pronghorn life. It all began with a nature walk in an area where home builders are hard at work converting prairie into an expanded neighborhood. I immediately developed a passion for keeping track of what the pronghorn herd was up to and possibly finding their shed horn or bone artifacts. In an eighteen month period, I completed 53 such pronghorn safari nature walks.

This book is designed to intertwine my observations with anecdotes of the adventures and surprises along the way. Abundant photographs and illustrations bring the story to life. As I convey the *who*, *what*, *where*, and *why* of pronghorn life, I share my cognitive, emotional, and spiritual impressions encountered during my "not so far from home" wilderness adventures. The goal of this literary work is to be succinct and fun to read, while blending a generous portion of scientific facts and personal observations. There are moments of wonderment and humor with occasionally poignant discoveries.

The audience members in mind are readers of all ages interested in Colorado wilderness adventure and encountering prairie wildlife, especially the pronghorn. Who are these majestic survivors hidden among the fringes of urban development? Did you know it is fun to collect pronghorn horns? Have you ever seen a jackalope? Come discover the mysteries of the pronghorn world during a time and place before urban expansion pushes the pronghorn further away. Enjoy!

– Professor Jim

Pronghorn on patrol.
"Where did these houses come from?"

"Greetings and welcome to the land of pronghorn!"

{ 1 }

The Adventure Begins!

Since moving to Colorado Springs in 1991, I have often seen herds of pronghorn antelope grazing in the surrounding grasslands. Pronghorn antelope were a daily sight on my drive to Schriever and Peterson Air Force bases during my service in the United States Air Force and later as a government contractor. In high school, my class would study Native American cave drawings depicting antelope hunts, an example shown in Figure 1. Growing up on the east coast in Pennsylvania, the pronghorn was and still is known as a symbol of the great American West – the famed American frontier of the Great Plains, the Rocky Mountains, and the Southwest. This was a place far away from city life, where history comes alive, and dreams can come true.

In 2020, I took an interest in observing pronghorn close up, studying their habits, behaviors, movements, and artifacts such as footprints, droppings, skeletal remains, and shed horns. I made other wildlife observations such as blooming cactuses, prowling coyotes, sprinting jack rabbits, soaring eagles, perching red tail hawks, and the fluttering of various small birds. The serenity and quiet of the seemingly endless and timeless grassland, a feeling of insignificance and smallness within the harsh and vast outdoors of God's immense and pristine creation, was of particular awe. The thought that pronghorn only live to about 10 years in the wild brought to mind how quickly our time on Earth

Figure 1. Ancient Pronghorn Petroglyph
Petroglyphs from Buckskin Gulch in Southern Utah exemplify how the Native Americans of the American Southwest revered and hunted pronghorn.

Figure 2. Family Adventurists and Finding Horns
From left to right are wife LaDonna, son Benjamin, and brother Don.

is fleeting – what are we to do in this short time? Several family members have joined me on safari, shown proudly with their horn finds in Figure 2.

Above all else, exploring pronghorn presented a life opportunity. For example, in *Built for Speed: A Year in the Life of Pronghorn*, author John Byers originally from upstate New York spent many years observing pronghorn by traveling to the remote northwest prairies of the National Bison Range in western Montana. I had a rare and unique opportunity to study a pronghorn herd in my own Colorado neighborhood, although the rapid housing development would quickly diminish this opportunity – the time was now!

Surprisingly, pronghorn thrive very close to human populations as the battle for prairie acreage is waged and repeatedly won by the bulldozer. The pronghorn live their daily lives and thrive in any open grassland, farmland, or cow pasture along the Colorado Front Range. As farm and ranch land gave way to housing developments, the pronghorn enjoy hanging around in ***their*** territory right up until the moment houses are built.

After all, the pronghorn were the first to mark their territory, as discussed later. Many of my safari observations came from pronghorn in a new housing development where families were moving in, just south of the thick pine tree groves in Black Forest, Colorado. The tan areas shown in Google Map "Satellite" view in Figure 3 were heavily populated by local herds, while Figures 4-6 show pronghorn in action on the ground in these areas.

Introducing the *who*, *what*, *where*, *why* and *how* have been touched upon thus far. In the pages ahead, I will expound in word and picture some of the detailed observations and discoveries during my pronghorn safaris.

Figure 3. Aerial Suburban Map and Adjacent Pronghorn Territory
The green arrow shows a distance of 1 mile. Pronghorn thrive right alongside housing development areas. See new housing development roads in bulldozed areas south of the dark-colored, forested Black Forest at the top of the map.

Figure 4. Confused Pronghorn Traverses a Construction Home Site
Pronghorn have been seen hanging around in their territory right up until the moment houses are built. See the pronghorn standing in a house lot and the unpaved road with curb visible in the foreground.

Figure 5. Pronghorn at Twilight
A pronghorn overlooks his past home prairieland, now overrun by home builders and bulldozers.

Figure 6. Pronghorn Roaming Once-Familiar Territory
These beautiful pronghorn pictures were taken from my car, parked on a newly constructed unpaved road in the newly built neighborhood. Pronghorn are not afraid of cars. If a human was standing there, the pronghorn would stay much further away.

Figure 6, part 2.

{ 2 }

What's a Pronghorn? Evolutionary Findings

A pronghorn antelope, also known as a pronghorn, is a deer-like animal thriving in the American West semi-desert, grassland wilderness, or *steppe*. See Figure 7 for pictures to compare elk (710 – 730 lbs), deer (150 – 300 lb), and pronghorn (88 – 140 lbs).

Figure 7. Elk, Deer vs. Pronghorn
Pronghorn on the far right has fibrous horns, not bone antlers like elk on the far left and deer in the center.

The pronghorn is a unique animal. They are deer-like animals that prefer to be in open grassland as opposed to hiding in protective forests and thickets. Like deer and members of the Ruminantia animal family, pronghorn enjoy lying in the field chewing their cud, known as ruminating. Pronghorn only live in semi-arid plateaus and plains of the American West and are the fastest land animal except for the African cheetah. Evolution-wise, they are largely unchanged over the last 30,000 years – same animal, same horns, same fast speed. Most other animals have drastically changed or have gone extinct since then, so the pronghorn is an amazing survivor.[33] Some of the pronghorn's most distinguishing features are[26]:

- Hollow hair like tiny tubes which provides added insulation against the extreme heat and cold environments
- Padding in their hoofs which provides shock absorption at high speed
- Drink when water is available, but can go for weeks in arid terrain without it, getting moisture from their food
- Largest trachea for their body size among ungulates (hoofed animals), which enables breathing enough air to maintain top speeds
- Large protruding eyes for exceptionally acute vision and defense against predators; each eyeball is about 36 mm (1.4 inches) in diameter

The term ***pronghorn*** can be confusing. In conversations I have had with people from Colorado, Texas, California, Pennsylvania, and other locations, rarely has anyone heard of a pronghorn. More times than not, the response is, "What's a pronghorn?" People are much more familiar with the term ***antelope***. Why is that?

I have discovered three compelling reasons why pronghorn are more widely known as antelope. First off, their scientific name, *Antilocapraamericana*, means "American antelope-goat," even though they are not closely related to the various antelope in Africa.[30] The second big influence was the Lewis and Clark expedition in 1804. When discovering the new antelope-goat animal, Captain Lewis favored naming it *antelope* due to its legs like a deer and graceful fleetness.[31] And third, we all know the cowboy classic song *Home on the Range* which repeats, "where the deer and the antelope play" in its chorus.[17, 22] These three mental touchstones, rooted in the initial naming by Captain Lewis, greatly influenced the pronghorn to be called *antelope*.

So, if they were called antelope from the beginning, when did they begin calling them pronghorn? The pronghorn does look like many antelope species found in Africa, yet they are different enough to have their own taxonomic family, *Antilocapridae*.[36] The pronghorn was first officially described by taxonomist George Ord in 1815.[15] Unlike the horns of the family Bovidae, the pronghorn's horns are uniquely branched, hence the name pronghorn. The outer portion of the horn grows from the skin covering a bony core; skin covering a bony horn core is similar to the Giraffidae family. It turns out that even though the pronghorn first appear to be closely related to the deer or African antelope, their closest relative based on DNA analysis is the giraffe.[29a] See Figure 8 for a pronghorn-giraffe-antelope comparison. Therefore, "upon further review," as they say, the scientific taxonomist community adopted the name ***pronghorn***. As Brent Huffman put it, "The origin of the name pronghorn is fairly obvious when looking at mature males – their horns are forked."[18]

Looking back through prehistoric records, the pronghorn is the only remaining member of the Antilocapridae family. Fossils have been found of 13 other now extinct members of this zoological family, all of which lived in North America.[21] Extinct antilocaprid family members are found from the Miocene, Pliocene, and Pleistocene periods of fossil records across North America.[32] Compare present day male and female, Figure 9 with illustrations of the Ungulate Family Tree, skulls illustrations from prehistoric ancestors, and our "final four" shown in Figures 10-12.

The group has a fossil record dating to the Miocene, about 20 million years ago.[3] During its history, the Antilocapridae has included a variety of species, some of which had multiple and bizarre horns.

Figure 8. Pronghorn Buck vs. Antelope, Giraffe

African antelope (gazelle) top, pronghorn left, giraffe right. Pronghorn and giraffe are close relatives based on most similar DNA.

In summary, as far back as 20 million years ago, there were at least ten pronghorn relatives that existed. Before the last Ice Age 11,000 years ago, there were four pronghorn species. After the last Ice Age, the mass extinctions of mammoths, saber-toothed tigers, and many other species occurred. Only the Antilocapra survived from the pronghorn family. Bones of modern pronghorn Antilocapra up to 10,000 years old have been found in California's La Brea Tar Pits.[30]

Figure 9. Pronghorn Buck with Horns and Doe
Bucks are about 10% bigger than does. (Photo credit, Alison Hardenburgh, Northern Desert Photography)

Figure 9 part 2

Does have very small or no horns, just bumps (photo credit, Jasmine A. Szczur)

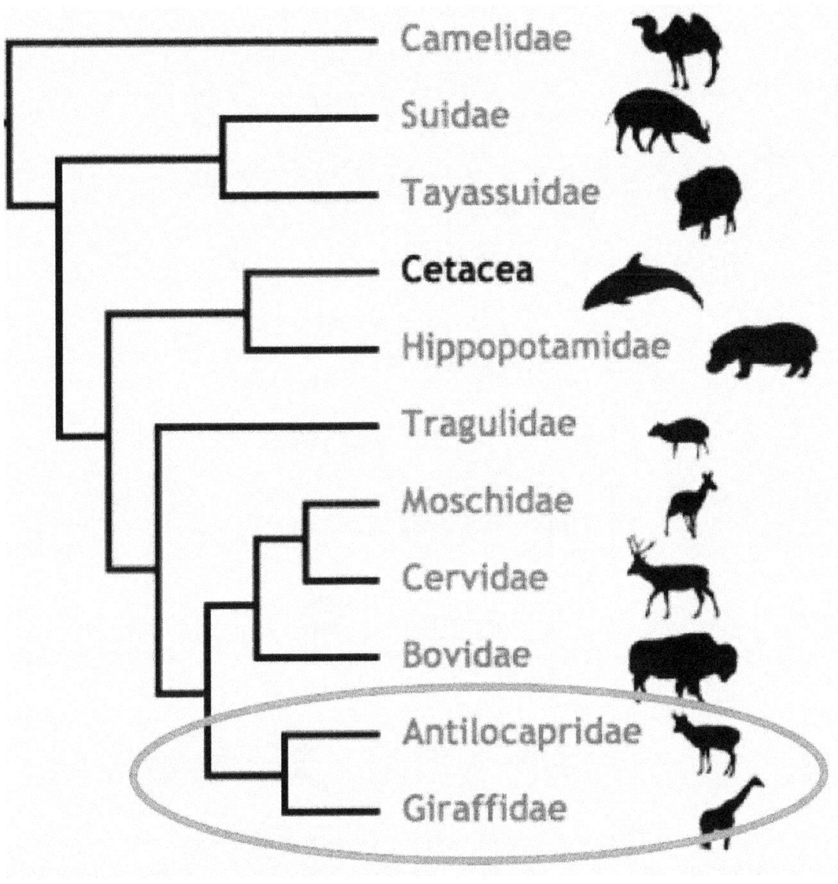

Figure 10. Ungulate Family Tree

The pronghorn and giraffe cousin are shown closely related in the family tree. Wow, did you know dolphin is a member of the ungulate family of hoofed animals?!

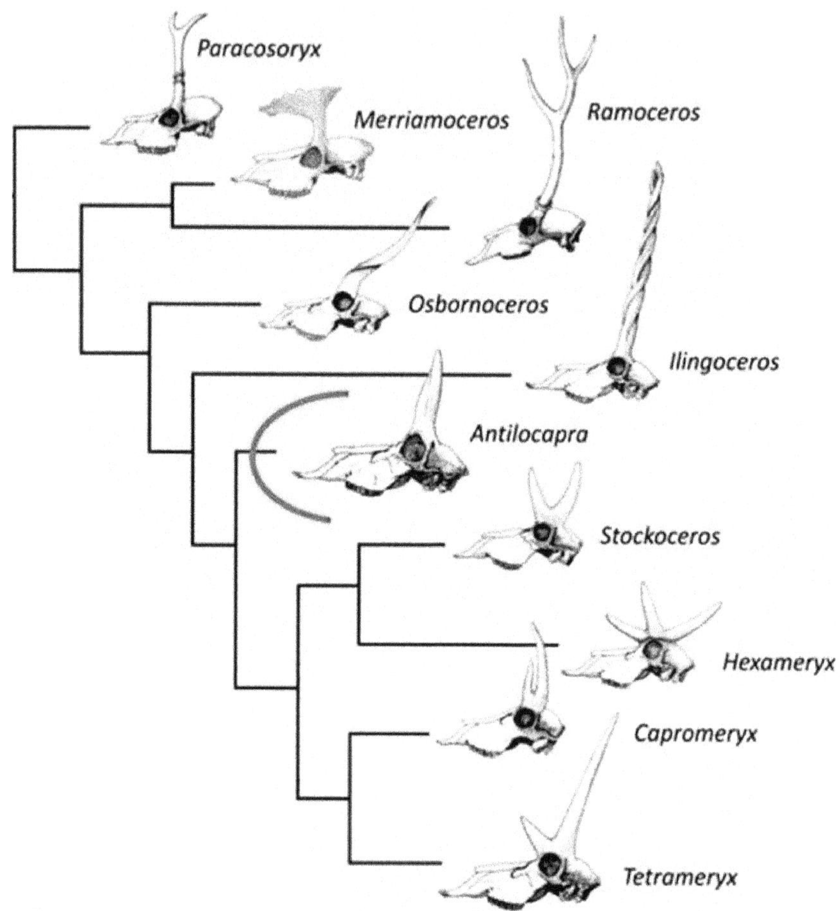

Figure 11. Prehistoric Pronghorn Ancestors

Note the relative sizes. Antilocapra, the modern pronghorn, is shown in the middle. Of the ten pronghorn relatives from 20 million years ago, only four pronghorn relatives survived up to the final Ice Age 11,000 years ago. Today, only the modern pronghorn, Antilocapra, has survived.

Figure 12. Tule Springs Prehistoric Pronghorn

Derived from pronghorn relative fossils found at Tule Springs Fossil Beds and La Brea tar pits, we have illustrations from left to right: Stockoceros, Antilocapra (modern pronghorn), Tetrameryx, Capromeryx.

Trophy-sized horns on display at the Denver Museum of Nature & Science.

{ 3 }

It's All About the Horns, PRONG-Horns

The pronghorn horns are uniquely different from those of other horned animals and are completely different from antlers. For example, elk and deer have antlers which grow from a pair of bony structures called pedicles on either side of the frontal skull bone. Antler bone grows from velvet, a skin that brings blood flow to enable antlers to grow, Figure 13. Each year, antlers grow from spring to fall seasons and naturally fall off, shedding in March. The annual antler growth cycle repeats.

In stark contrast, pronghorn do not have antlers, but horns. All horned animals have horns comprised of a bone core plus a hard yet fibrous keratin outer portion, the same material as hair, fingernails, and toenails. Figure 14 shows the horns of many animals. Horns do not grow directly from the bone but from connective tissue between the bone and the keratin outer portion.[35]

Now that the "finer points" of horn structure have been described, from here out the pronghorn's keratin outer horn, sometimes called a horn sheath, is simply referred to as the pronghorn's horn. As such, the horns of the pronghorn are uniquely different in two specific ways from other horned animals: (1) their horns shed each year, and (2) each individual horn has two points rather than one. Take notice in

Figure 13. Deer with Velvet Covering Growing Bone Antlers
Antlers are bone growths fed with blood supplied by the velvet outer skin. Horns are not bone, but made of keratin.

Figure 15 that the horn is hollow as viewed from the base due to the spiked bone structure with a unique skin layer in lieu of connective tissue from which the horn grew. More views of horns are shown in Figures 16-17.

One of the artifacts I found during my pronghorn safaris (observed, not hunted) was an intact skull with remarkable features, shown in Figure 18. The hallmark features of a male pronghorn skull are its large eye sockets and horn-bone structures projecting vertically and about 45-degrees outwardly from the top of each eye socket. Their large eyes are on either side of their skull, giving the pronghorn a 300-degree field of view and movement detection at a range of 4 miles.[30]

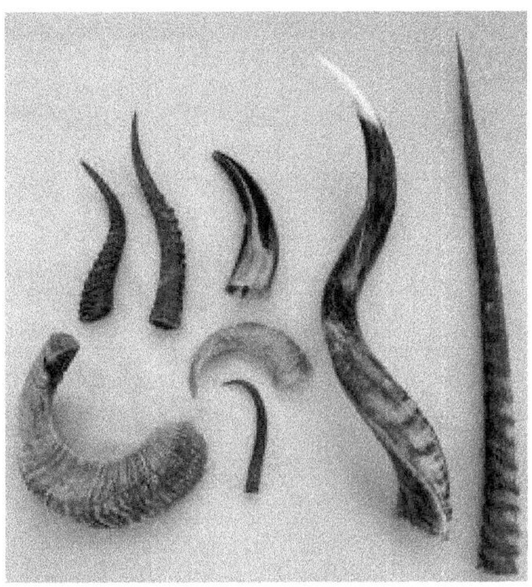

Figure 14. Horns Have Different Shapes and Sizes

Big Horn Sheep are an excellent example of permanent horns that grow larger throughout its life. Pronghorn are the only horned animal that shed their horns each year.

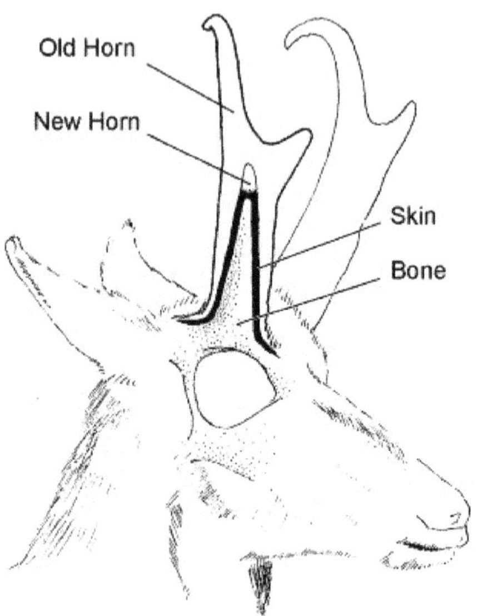

Figure 15. Horn of a Pronghorn with Bony Core and Skin Covering
The horn is hollow as viewed from the base due to the spiked bone structure.

Figure 16. Pronghorn Buck and Doe in Their Green Spring Paradise

Figure 17. Matching Set of Pronghorn Horns
Horns of the pronghorn are unique in that they fall off every November, are made of fibrous keratin, not bone, and have two points, not one.

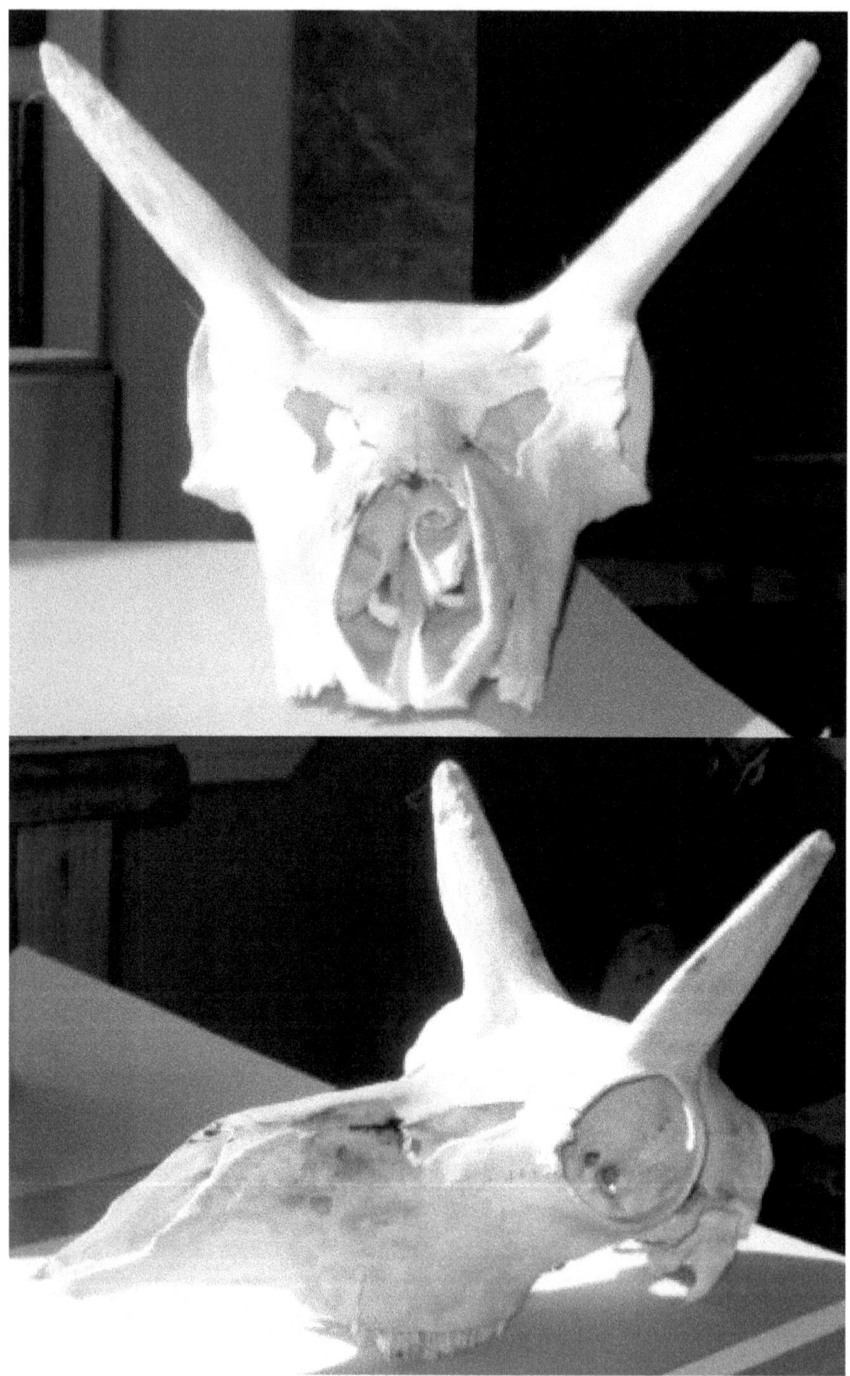

Figure 18. Pronghorn Skull Photos

Of particular note is the nostril sinus cavity bone structure, two spiral-shaped, wafer-thin bones within the sinus cavity. This spiral nostril bone structure allows olfactory tissue spread over a huge surface area resulting in the pronghorn's acute sense of smell.

In the female pronghorn skull shown in Figure 19, top, the jaw tooth structure is similar to the female deer shown in Figure 19, bottom.

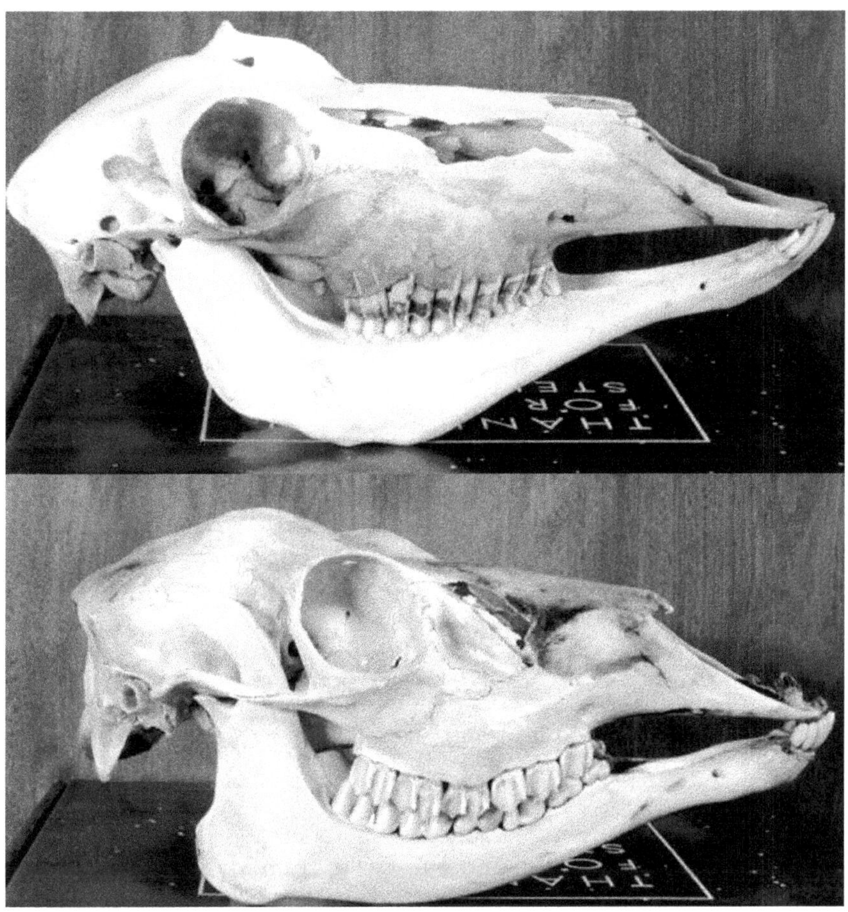

Figure 19. Pronghorn skull top, and deer skull bottom

Both skulls have striking similarities, but are different in that the pronghorn has side-looking eyes, small female horn nubs, and round lower jaw line. The deer has a square jaw line.

Both have opposing skull-to-jaw grinding molars that fit perfectly like puzzle pieces. Some pronghorn skulls I recovered had baby teeth and submerged molars which could be used to determine accurate pronghorn age. Pronghorn are similar to deer in brain cavity and other features, but differ in other ways, as in the pronghorn side-looking and the deer's forward looking eye sockets. Eye field of view was captured as shown below in Figure 19, part 2, showing a pronghorn's posterior-view while jumping a fence. Notice both eyes are in view! Pronghorn seem to embody the expression, "you must have eyes in the back of your head."

Figure 19, part 2, Posterior view of pronghorn head shows direct eye line of sight, both eyes!

Only male pronghorn have large horns and supporting skull structure. Some sources incorrectly claim that the male pronghorn bone is pronged resulting in a pronged outer horn, but that is not the case. The bone is in the shape of a single wedged spike with no prong. The main horn grows vertically and outwardly from above the eye socket, and then as the horn grows, it curves back and inward to varying degrees on individual animals, as shown in Figure 20.

The forward-thrusting prong on a horn varies in size, shape, and inward curvature depending on the individual animal. Some prongs are triangular, while others are curved and pointed like a rose thorn.

Figure 20. Annual Growth of Pronghorn Horns

Each year in November, the male's new horn pushes off and sheds the old horn. This is the perfect time to hunt for shed horns! The new horns grow through the winter and are fully developed by May.

Sharpness and size of the prong vary across different horns. Inward curvature of the prong can have no curvature to extreme "ice cream scoop" curvature. Even a slight outward curvature is possible.

Some prongs and horn tips were chipped or worn down indicating significant combat action in the field. Many variations in horn shape and size are shown in Figure 21. Make no mistake; an overall large size makes the most impressive horn! There is a hunters' guide to assign a score for a pair of horns based on a series of measurements including overall length, girth at several locations, and prong length. A horn, especially a trophy-sized horn, is a sight to behold considering it has traveled with the buck for one year, one tenth of its lifespan – where did it travel during all that time? What were the temperatures and weather conditions? What predators did it battle? How many other pronghorns looked at the horn to determine social status or assess mating potential? The horn is the pronghorn's crown, his defensive weapon, his calling card among the herd as well as other animals on the prairie. Each horn has its own story, and the horn's unique variations add to the beauty and intrigue of each individual horn.

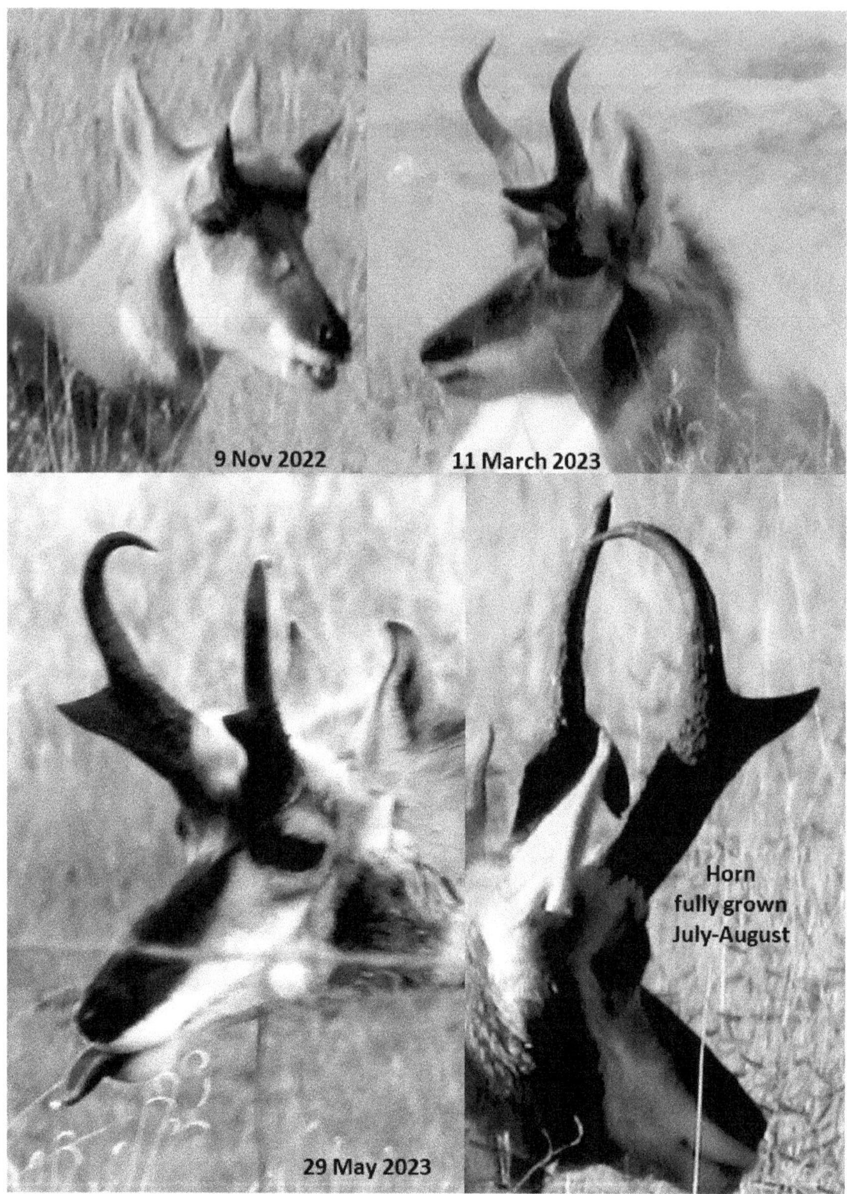

Shown above is a more detailed sequence of photographs illustrating the phases of pronghorn horn growth occurring every year. In November, horn sheaths are shed allowing the new horn underneath to become visible and grow. Through May, horn tips continue to grow and curl. The horn base continues growing through August increasing overall height of the horn. The biggest horns impress the females and entice joust challenges among the males during the late September-early October rut.

See pronghorn with both horns (top) and with one horn missing (lower left). I found the missing right horn (lower right) about 20 feet from where I took this picture, and it is now in my 2022 collection. When the two pictures are compared, you can see the horn matches! When a horn falls off in the November timeframe, it is pushed off by the new horn growing underneath, like a baby tooth getting pushed out by its new adult tooth. The newly developing keratin horn is spike shaped like its bony core and will rapidly grow from December until fully grown in size, curved points, and prong by May.

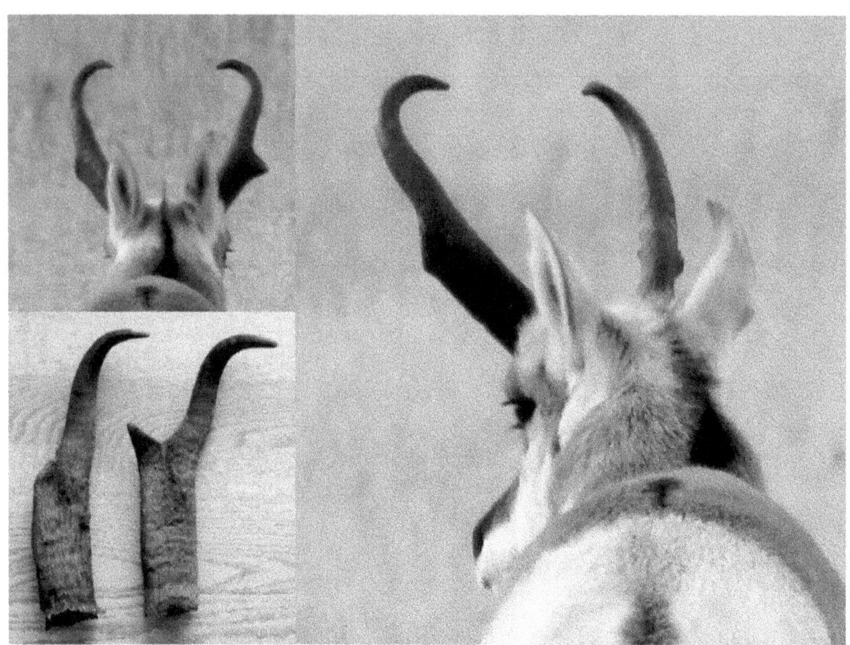

Sometimes, a mature male pronghorn may have a prong missing from his horn. No, they do not snap off in combat, but just grow that way on occasion. I saw a pronghorn with the same missing prong two years in a row, so a missing prong on a given horn could be genetically programmed for that specific animal. Just another fascinating horn growth uniqueness.

Figure 21. Horn Size and Shape Uniqueness

A pronghorn with a distinctly unique set of horns is shown. Note the freakish, downward pointed prong on the right. I named him "Left Hook" and photographed him in August 2022.

The neighborhood pronghorn herd.

{ 4 }

Habitat and Conservation

Pronghorn and their evolutionary ancestors lived in North America for millions of years, surviving Ice Age climatic change, as well as fierce predation by the now-extinct American cheetah. Today, cheetahs only live in Africa. Prior to the westward expansion of the 1800s, pronghorn population was over 40 million – more pronghorn than Bison.[30] By the 1920s, hunting pressure decimated total pronghorn population to a minuscule 13,000 animals. Due to aggressive conservatory measures starting with President Franklin Roosevelt's executive order in 1936 creating a 549,000-acre pronghorn sanctuary tract, pronghorn populations began an immediate recovery. Through the protection of habitat and hunting restrictions, total pronghorn population today is at 1 million.[23]

A map of the pronghorn range and habitat is shown in Figure 22.[18] Herds merge and disperse throughout their annual cycle. The merging of herds is particularly striking in areas where they migrate in the winter and spring, such as Wyoming's Grand Teton and Sublette County areas where fossil evidence of the 180-mile migration route show 10 thousand years of seasonal use.[40] Pronghorn and mule deer populations plummeted when urban and farm development blocked migration paths. Urban development and fences used on farm and ranchland resulted in pronghorn habitat loss or fragmentation blocking vital migration routes. However, a second major success story for

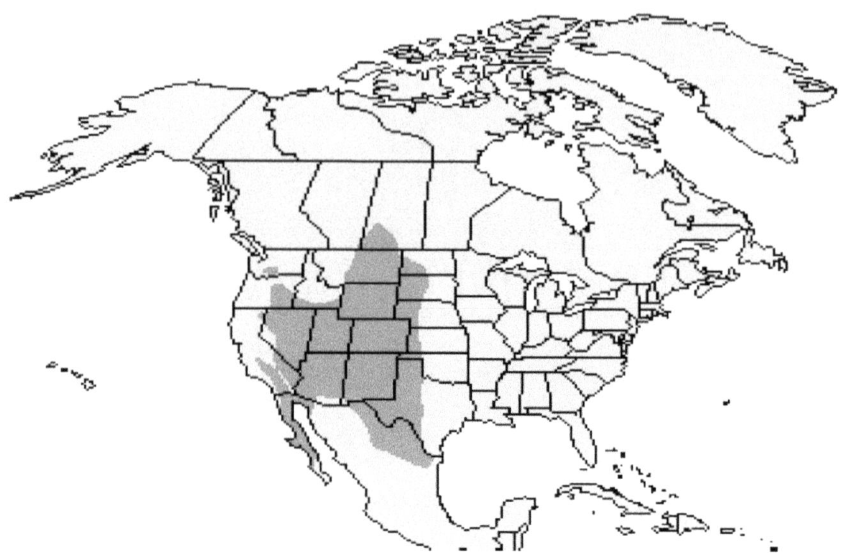

Figure 22. Pronghorn Range and Habitat

pronghorn occurred in 2008. This is when the U.S. Forest Service officially designated a conservation area called, "The Path of the Pronghorn." This project contiguously protected a large herd migratory route from Grand Teton National Park (summer locale) to Rock Springs, Wyoming (winter locale) 180 miles away. The project's pronghorn overpass is shown in Figure 23. The route was previously obstructed with fencing and housing development threatening herd survival.[42] Pictures and illustrations concerning pronghorn migration, pronghorn traversing fences, and the design of wildlife-friendly fences are shown in Figures 24-28.

Deer and pronghorn prefer to go under a fence, rather than over. U.S. Bureau of Land Management's Spokane District in concert with other western state agencies have been pursuing an effort to make wildlife-friendly fences by specifying the distance between the barbed and smooth wires, as shown in Figure 28.

The best wildlife friendly fence is highly visible and allows easy jump over or slip under without getting gouged or injured by sharp barbed wire. The bottom wire should be 18 inches off the ground

Figure 23. Pronghorn Crossing over Highway in Wyoming

Figure 24. The Herd Thriving in Winter

Figure 25. Pronghorn Herd Crossing Under a Fence

Figure 26. Pronghorn Jumping Over a Fence

Pronghorn are capable of jumping fences, but same as deer, they prefer to crawl under fences lest they risk injury and eventual death in the harsh wilderness fraught with predators.

Pronghorn gets "air."

Figure 27. Pronghorn and Deer Prefer to Crawl Under Fences

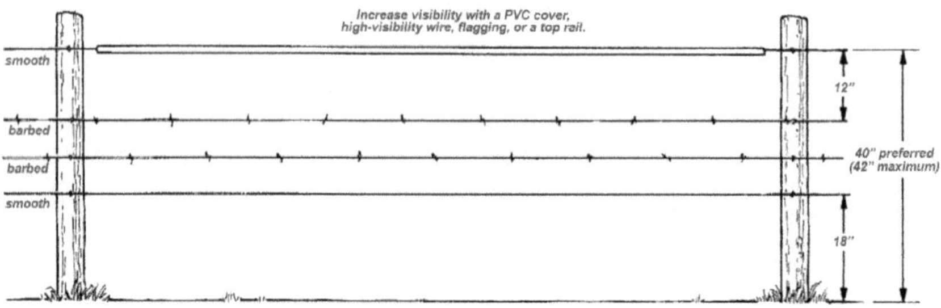

Figure 28. Wildlife Friendly Fence Design

Fences checker the pronghorn and deer habitat across the western grasslands often causing serious injury to these animals. This design provides space for crawling under or leaping over without injury while keeping horses, cows, and other farm and ranch animals securely penned in.

because a lot of times pronghorn and mule deer prefer to go under fences. The middle two strands should be closer together in order to leave more room below the top wire. If a pronghorn or deer jump over the fence, and a leg hits the top wire, there will be enough space so that the two wires do not tangle and trap the leaping animal's foot. Tight fences are safer than loose wires that tangle more easily. By properly combining smooth wire and barbed wire, the fence controls livestock and allows safe passage for pronghorn, deer, and elk.[14]

{ 5 }

Fawns Are so Cute!

Fawns arrive in the springtime and are so cute! I took the photographs in Figure 29 from about 100-yards away. Even at a young age of one month, this little guy was all by himself and popped up out of the grass when I unknowingly walked nearby. Being so close to a beautiful baby pronghorn was totally unexpected. It is standard practice for a mom to stay up to a mile away between feedings to draw predator attention away from the fawn that stays low, quiet, and motionless in the grass.

Figure 29 Pronghorn Fawn

The fawn kept its distance, but turned and walked toward me following its natural curious instinct to check me out. After the fawn trotted away, I examined the soil where the fawn was standing and found its cute baby hoof prints, shown in Figure 30. Then, I departed the area as to minimize the intrusion. Figure 31 shows a photograph of a family with three fawns. More fawns are shown in Figure 32.

Figure 29, part 2. Fawn just keeps looking at me.
This little guy is NOT camera shy!

Figure 29, part 3.
"Is this my good side?"

Figure 30. Fawn Foot Prints
Two footprints are cast in mud with car keys shown for scale.

Time to learn to run!

New fawn with mom in June.

Figure 31. Three Fawn with Parents

The pronghorn herd is teaming with new life! Here we have 9 fawns and 2 moms. After a few weeks or so after birth, fawns are gathered into little "day care" groups.

Figure 32. Close Up of Fawn
Mom is still sporting her shaggy winter coat.

While prancing with the pronghorn herd and among their newborn fawns, a host of other animal and plant life emerges in splendor in late springtime. The horned lizards and blooming cacti are two such examples. The horned lizard is shown in Figure 33 is also known as a horny toad or a horned toad. It likes to remain motionless and rely on its remarkable camouflage to avoid detection by predators. The pincushion cactus has bright pink flowers, while the yellow prickly pear cactus has beautiful yellow blooms, Figure 34.

Photographs of a bird's nest with baby birds and an eagle in flight shown in Figures 35-36 showcase bird activity on the prairie.

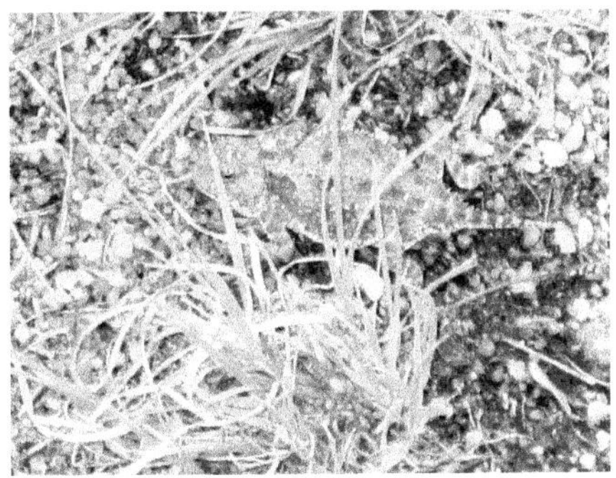

Figure 33. Horned Lizard

Figure 34. Blooming Cacti

Figure 35. Bird Nest in a Tuft of Grass

Figure 36. Eagle

I would be remiss if I did not make mention of the astonishing jackrabbit. On a number of occasions as I was hiking across the prairie, I would be startled by a sudden noise of an animal springing from its hiding place and gliding at lightning speed across the terrain for about 100-200 yards. I have witnessed jackrabbits cuddled up and holding their position quiet and still in the brush as I unknowingly approached. Jackrabbits are well camouflaged and freeze their position when approached making them completely undetectable. Then suddenly from as close as 5 feet away, a burst of noise and sudden movement would occur without warning! I would immediately freeze and look toward the noise and motion. At close proximity, jackrabbits seem rather large. After they launch from the brush like a racehorse bursting from its starting gate, their explosive gallop becomes a quiet whisper. The jackrabbit alternates between sprinting with rapid leg movement and gracefully leaping, their flying posture briefly frozen in air, shown in Figure 37. These amazingly large rabbits of the prairie, with their long, erect ears as they glide and bound across the prairie, definitely resemble a miniature pronghorn! I am confident that this remarkable resemblance to a pronghorn-antelope in flight is what has given rise to the legendary creature, ... The Jackalope!

Figure 37. Jackrabbit in Flight
Sure looked like a Jackalope,... and then it was gone in a blink of an eye!

Springtime is not without its dangers. There are coyotes on the prowl looking for fawns that might make a tasty meal. As shown in Figure 38, I witnessed a portion of the herd gather like a football team to confront a passing coyote. As an organized team, they are uncontested in chasing off certain threats. Other times, several males will gather the entire herd before they all start running together across the prairie to a safer location. A pronghorn herd taking flight and running as an entire herd is an amazing sight to see as shown in Figure 39 and is strikingly quiet considering thirty-five or more individual animals are sprinting at sixty miles per hour.

Figure 38. Herd of Pronghorn Chasing Off a Coyote

Figure 39. Pronghorn on the Move

Caught these six among a herd of 35 stampeding across the grassland (top), predators shown (bottom).

A lonely house on the Colorado prairie illustrates timeless wilderness.

{ 6 }

The Timeless Wilderness and Wandering Thoughts

During my pronghorn safaris, I often encountered various rubbish left over from travelers or tenants of the land from years or even centuries gone by. I pause and ponder the possibility that a piece of metal or glass would just sit out on the prairie in plain view and untouched for many years. The semi-arid climate of the Colorado prairie results in dry soil with sparse grass and vegetation growth preserving such materials and keeping them plainly visible for a long time. In contrast, the east coast with its generous rainfall and lush vegetation growth, results in such articles vanishing from view. Tree and shrub growth, piles of leaves, rust and decay, year after year tend to erase any such evidence of human presence.

During one of my safaris, I came across an old, homemade-looking, bright blue glass bottle with embossed labeling that read, "Bromo-Seltzer, Emerson Drug Co., Baltimore MD," Figure 40. This brought to mind a previous occasion when I found a 1908 penny in a similar prairie environment, also shown. These discoveries struck me as fascinating and extraordinary for me to have found such man made articles in the random wilderness.

Coincidentally, both articles originated from the same time period. Upon returning home that day, I went online and researched the history of the Bromo-Seltzer bottle. I discovered Bromo-Seltzer was invented in 1888 and produced by the Emerson Drug Company of Baltimore, Maryland, as a hangover remedy. The blue bottle was made in 1907-1910 time frame.[20] Bromo-Seltzer and other bromide tranquilizer substances were taken off the U.S. market in 1975 due to their toxicity. In a push to make a unique, attractive packaging for marketing, the decorative cobalt-blue Bromo-Seltzer embossed glass bottle was part of the Bromo-Seltzer product line branding. My discovery of the antique bottle and penny are tangible reminders of how tidbits of human habitation can sit there in the Colorado wilderness, untouched for many, many years with little corrosion.

Figure 40. Frontier Artifacts Discovered
Emerson's Bromo-Seltzer bottle (5-inch tall) and 1908 penny (same size as our modern penny). Both artifacts were found in the grassland wilderness of Colorado.

"This prairie has a lot of pronghorn family history," I pondered as I considered the passage of time and how unchanged pronghorn territory is that blankets across the wild prairie land of Colorado. Imagine living back in time, when Emerson's Bromo-Seltzer was the hottest, new, must-have item for your medicine cabinet, especially in the frontier land of Colorado. In the early 1900's, Bromo-seltzer was sold from wagons, a moment in time captured in Figure 41.

Figure 41. Emerson's Bromo-Seltzer Wagon (circa 1910)

My mind could not help but wonder how many generations of pronghorn lived between 1900 and 2020; at least 40 generations given a pronghorn generation is three years compared to their full ten year lifespan.

The pronghorn lifespan of ten years[4] roughly compares to a human eighty year average life expectancy in the United States.[9] As humans, especially those in our latter years, time seems to fly by. How often do we overhear conversations of someone saying, "Oh my, summer is over," or, "Wow, time to put out Christmas decorations again – where did the year go?!" How much faster must time go by for the pronghorn, with each season averaging one-tenth of their life span?

Yes, one year is roughly equivalent to 8 human years. A prong-horn doe can have young as early as two years old. A four year old pronghorn may be considered in the prime of life, as is a thirty-two year old human. Hunters report that the largest horns are from three or four year old bucks. Perhaps the eight year old pronghorn is contemplating retirement, whatever that looks like in the pronghorn world. And the nine year old pronghorn buck may be viewed as the grand-daddy of the herd. What is it that makes the pronghorn think back on their life and reflect: Have I lived a full life? Perhaps these deep thoughts border on silliness. All the same, as I roamed in the serene wilderness in conversation with God and in awe of His creation, I would ponder these things. A pronghorn's relatively short lifespan, yet, not living life in a hurry, and how it would be to live life as a pronghorn – definitely a subject on which to ruminate!

{ 7 }

Behavior – What Do Pronghorn Do?

One of my first impressions on that introductory pronghorn safari on November 26, 2020, was the striking curiousness of pronghorn. From about 300 yards away, the herd spotted my approach. Three bucks broke away from the main herd of twenty and slowly walked toward me, seemingly to check me out.I imagine this pronghorn envoy was on a mission to determine if I was a threat and to assess how much distance from me the herd should maintain. After the pronghorn envoy closed in to about 150 yards away, they stopped, stared, and seemed to make thoughtful assessment of me. An occasional snort could be heard. After their curiosity was satisfied and their assessment complete, they turned and casually walked back to the herd. The herd gathered and all at once broke into a trot, gathering again in an area about a quarter of a mile away. My impression is that pronghorn are amazingly curious and fearless, controlling their surroundings with their alertness, communication, and unmatched speed to escape surprise attacks on the herd. Herd movements guided by several bucks are shown in Figures 42-43.

Pronghorn are social and like to cluster in herds of about twenty. In December of 2020, I witnessed three such herds cluster into one large herd of about fifty-five which gathered and broke away into a

Figure 42. Are You Lookin' at Me?

Figure 43. Nothing to See Here; Move Along Please...
Three bucks stand guard staring down the intruder, while the main herd moves away.

full run for about a half mile across the grassland. It appeared this was a response to my presence, although it seemed like they enjoyed executing their little fire drill more than it being an actual fear response. It seemed they liked to find an excuse to gather and run into a full-speed stampede. It was fun to watch the herd run in a high-speed, follow-the-leader mode.

As if that wasn't amazing enough, the herd eventually drifted in a loop, approached me again at about 200 yards away and broke into another stampede. This time, they ran right past me in the opposite direction completing a full circular route within the prairie enclave. What fun for me and the pronghorn on that beautiful sunny Colorado day!

While observing the pronghorn, I have witnessed remarkable episodes of leadership behavior. As I was traversing a valley approaching the pronghorn herd, the herd was moving to the right walking toward an adjacent hillock. A large, seemingly wise, pronghorn buck with big horns was bringing up the rear, as I have often observed. This time, as the herd calmly walked toward the hillock to the right, this great stag leader of the herd held back and then turned and started walking to the left. He was diverting my attention from the herd so I would follow him in the opposite direction, which I did for a while. I was intrigued that he would selflessly choose to draw away a potential threat from the main herd to provide for their safety.

Another behavior pattern I have observed among the herd involves exploration of surrounding territory by a single buck or small group of three or four bucks. The females seem to prefer staying among the herd, while the males seem to exhibit protective, exploratory, on-watch behaviors, to include challenging potential threats. Often, male pronghorn will climb to the top of a hillock to get a more distant view of the surrounding area and demonstrate vocal displays and threatening stares to confront intruders. The buck in Figure 44 is giving his "crow call" to signal his presence.

I observed pronghorn on patrol with their eyes, ears, and smell senses fully engaged at maximum range. Upon seeing something of concern, such as an intruder or possible threat, the pronghorn would message back to others nearby using their keen eyes, ears, and sense of smell. First, pronghorn communications include the odor of their musk or excrement associated with marking territory. Additionally, a buck's dark cheek patches are a source of musk for marking territory with odor by rubbing their cheeks on fence posts or shrubs. Second, sight cueing is exhibited in the form of alert, commanding posture on

Figure 44. Pronghorn Blowing or Giving Its "Crow-Call" Sound
A rare picture of a pronghorn blowing or giving its "crow-call" sound.

a ridge or the erecting of their bright white rump hair similar to a porcupine erecting its quills as a defense mechanism.

These bright white "warning flags" can be seen at a long distance. Additionally, the cotton-white rump patch serves as a beacon so the herd can stick together when fleeing, especially at dawn, dusk, or night. Third, pronghorn have verbal communication. Pronghorn will give a single snort or blowing noise. Alternately, the pronghorn can give what sounds similar to a single crow-call sound. Any of these sound signals provide effective communication which carries for a long distance to warn other pronghorn. To hear pronghorn snort and crow call, go to this URL: https://youtu.be/y6_KxG_xFM4 or search the Internet on "pronghorn warning sound."

The senior buck is on watch.

{ 8 }

Marking Territory – It All Comes Out in the End!

Pronghorn are territorial and like to mark their territory. Pronghorn mark their territory for several reasons: (1) to help a pronghorn keep track of their territory, (2) to mark their favorite trails, and (3) to warn other pronghorn that they are crossing into another pronghorn's territory which could lead to a fight if it is rutting season.

I have seen heavily marked spots along trails where an opening in the fence exists, as well as on the crest of a hill where trails merge, and also in areas of high traffic. These points of reference provide a navigational framework for the pronghorn and other animals and often define where the pronghorn like to spend most of their time.

Mature pronghorn bucks often scent mark with urine and scat in a ritualistic manner, known as Sniff-Paw-Urinate-Defecate, or SPUD.[33] On occasion, I have personally witnessed pronghorn marking their territory in this way. Given I was looking at him, he was in turn looking back at me. As the pronghorn buck watched me, I saw him scraping the soil with his front hoof in preparation to mark his territory. He then stepped forward, then leaned forward and held that position while urinating. For his crescendo, another step forward and slight squat to defecate completed the territorial marking ceremony. A pronghorn buck in this squatting position is shown in Figure 45 with scat illustrated in Figures 46-47. On one occasion, I found the spot where all this occurred and captured a picture of the buck and his resulting "territory mark," shown in Figure 48. Trying not to get too graphic, I can say I held my hand out and felt the heat radiating off the fresh excrement like a warm coal from a camp fire.

"Wow, it doesn't get much fresher than that," I mused. It is remarkable how persistent and pronounced the territory markings are. I'm sure the readers will be relieved to know, I did not perform any smell or taste analysis. More pictures of scat and a video showing a buck mark his territory are found at the URL: https://youtu.be/x29HQwYR5fI or search the Internet for "pronghorn tracks and signs."

Figure 45. Pronghorn Marking His Territory
Pronghorn buck deposits scat after scraping the ground to mark his territory.

Normally, pronghorn scat is very dry, undoubtedly due to bodily water conservation. Scat can be compressed looking like a pine cone or crumbled to look like scattered coffee beans, as shown in Figure 47.

It was unusual when one time I saw extremely moist and bright green scat, shown in Figure 48. Similar deer scat is documented to vary with diet.[8] I likewise attribute the particularly moist and green pronghorn scat to be due to plentiful spring rain and lush vegetation in the pronghorn diet over the previous several weeks, but none the less is a topic for further research.

Figure 46. Pronghorn Territory or Trail Marking
Pronghorn scrape marks and deposits of scat are shown.

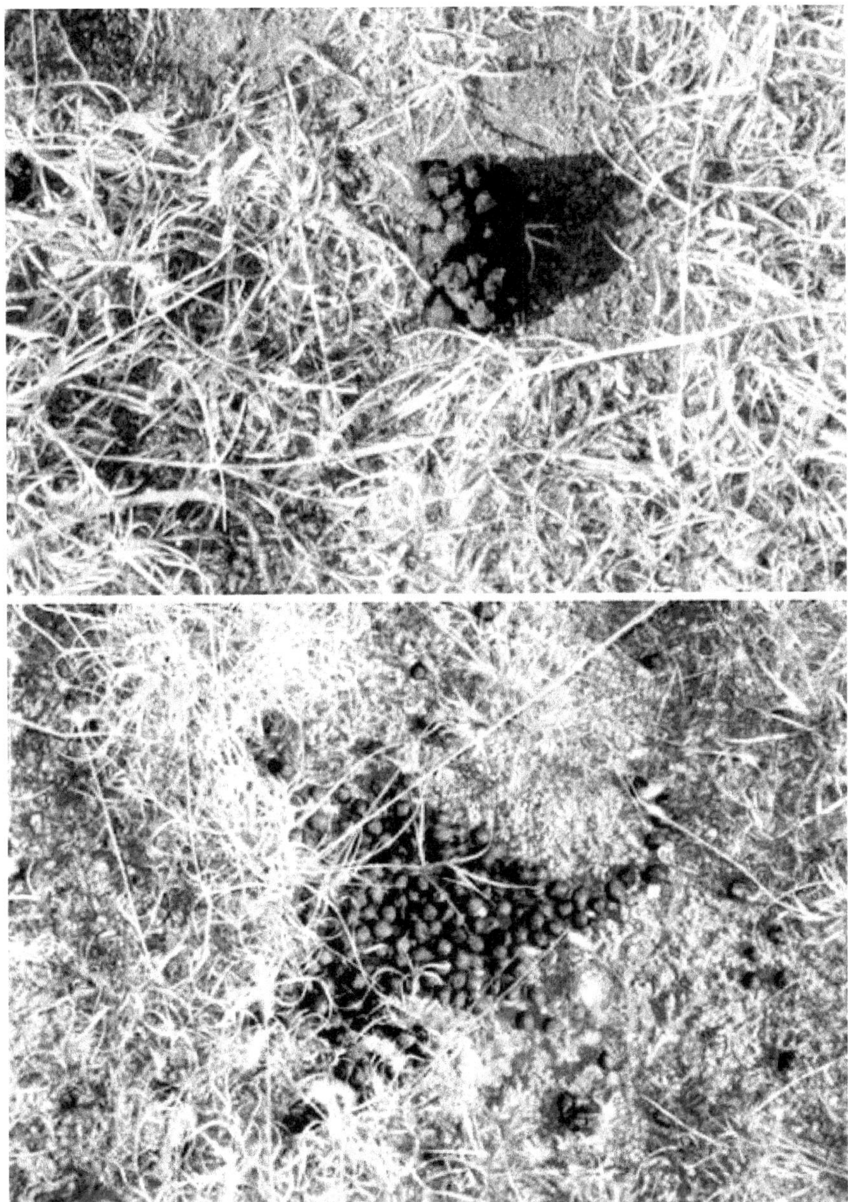

Figure 47. Pronghorn Scat Identification

Pronghorn scat is very dry. Scat can be compressed looking like a pine cone (top), or crumbled to look like scattered coffee beans (bottom).

Figure 48. Pronghorn and the Marking He Left

Yes, I watched the whole thing. The unusual excrement could have been diarrhea caused by sickness or simply the lush vegetation this time of year.

{ 9 }

Rut's That All About?!

Like deer, pronghorn males lock horns to determine dominance and who gets to mate with the females – this sparring-for-dominance behavior is called the rut, shown in Figure 49. In addition to defending territory to hold a harem of does, pronghorn bucks fight viciously and sometimes fatally during the rut.[24]

Figure 49. Pronghorn Locking Horns

Rutting behavior can start off as short-lived, low intensity, pushing and shoving matches to establish male dominance hierarchy from mid-August to mid-October.[10] Sparring matches may escalate to full-blown horn-locking fights near the peak of mating season in early October, Figure 50. Search the Internet for "pronghorn antelope fight rut" to find great video clips of pronghorn rut action, such as: https://youtu.be/tSVu5Kp5HOg or https://youtu.be/4k3pJSnvKsw. Wow, very impressive live-action video clips. What is all the fighting and rutting about? The buck must chase off the uninvited buck intruding on his harem of ten or more female pronghorn. A more peaceful YouTube video of a buck mingling with his harem is found at the link: https://youtu.be/Ex8k8Dw_Mzc or search the Internet for "pronghorn herd sound of nature".

My wife, LaDonna, and I witnessed two male pronghorn sparring and kicking up some serious dust on June 20, 2021. We witnessed unique behavior within the herd. While the two bucks were sparring, a third more senior buck dashed to the scene and appeared to break up the fight. Moments later, a coyote entered the scene and a group of five pronghorn teamed up to run him off, as there were still many vulnerable fawns in the vicinity in June. Could it be that the wise, senior buck knew it was not yet sparring season, but still time to focus on protecting fawns from coyotes? Observing these behaviors left me with an impression that pronghorn are highly observant and display a variety of complex social behavior.

The boys practice locking horns in June.

Figure 50. Pronghorn Rutting
(photo credit, Alison Hardenburgh, Northern Desert Photography)

Figure 50, part 2. "Show me what-cha got, big guy..."
These bucks are not playing!

Pronghorn snacking after a long day of rutting.

Who's next in the joust competition?

Horn find!

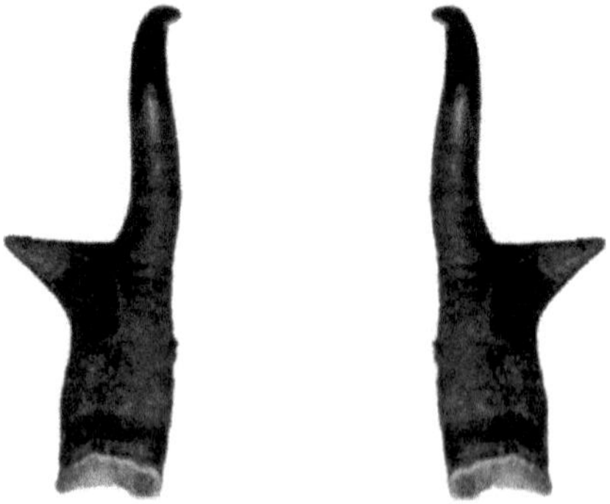

A matching set!

{ 10 }

Horn Hunting – It's a Thing!

Horn hunting is an exciting sport gaining in popularity for the outdoors man in all of us. It requires enjoying being outdoors, concentration, keen eyesight,and the stamina for walking many miles for most of the day. Many horns are illustrated in this chapter, but I have found that the chances of finding a horn on any given day are slim.

Some techniques improve your chances of finding a horn. When looking for horns, focus on curvature and points, not necessarily the whole horn. Chances are you may stumble on one right under your feet, so it's important to look everywhere. The best technique is to put in the miles, keep your eyes scanning, and to expect the unexpected.

Jessica Delorenzo said it well in her blog *Beginner's Guide to Shed Hunting*: Here's your chance to be a kid on an Easter egg hunt – except trade in the candy and backyards for horns and prairies.[12] Bob Humphrey offered great tips like how to spot bedding areas.[19] Techniques I have used are to spot a herd and observe them for a while, every few days for two weeks. Survey a given area to determine where the pronghorn hang out the most. Take note on where pronghorn may spend the night, their favorite feeding locations, and their commonly used trails or fence crossings. If one enjoys the outdoors and the serenity of the front-range wilderness, and is in good shape for long hikes,horn hunting will be great fun!

I have had lots of success hiking through areas where I have seen the herd shortly before and after horns disappear from the pronghorn bucks' heads, approximately late November into December. As you are hunting, keep a "mental search image" or mind picture such as a stick or hook portion of the horn in mind. Anything that vaguely looks like your mental search image could be a horn and is worth walking over and checking out. I was ecstatic when I found my first full-size male horn compared to the smaller female horns I had also found, shown in Figure 51. Ironically, the less-impressive female horns are much harder to find because they are smaller. My collection grew to 56 horns by March 2022, some shown in Figures 52-56. When observing a herd in November, it is time to keep closer attention to the ground when one starts noticing horns on the head of male pronghorn starting to disappear, as noted in Figure 57. Try to figure out where they were sleeping the night before, what trails were most heavily used recently, and what fence did they pass through for your best chance of striking it big!

Figure 51. My First Full-Size Horn Find

Figure 52. Horns of the Pronghorn, My 2020 Collection

Figure 53. Horns of the Pronghorn, My 2021 Collection

The horn on the far right is 10-inches top to bottom, shown by the green arrow. Horn base-to-tip length measured using a string is close to 15 inches on the largest horns. Green arrow, right.

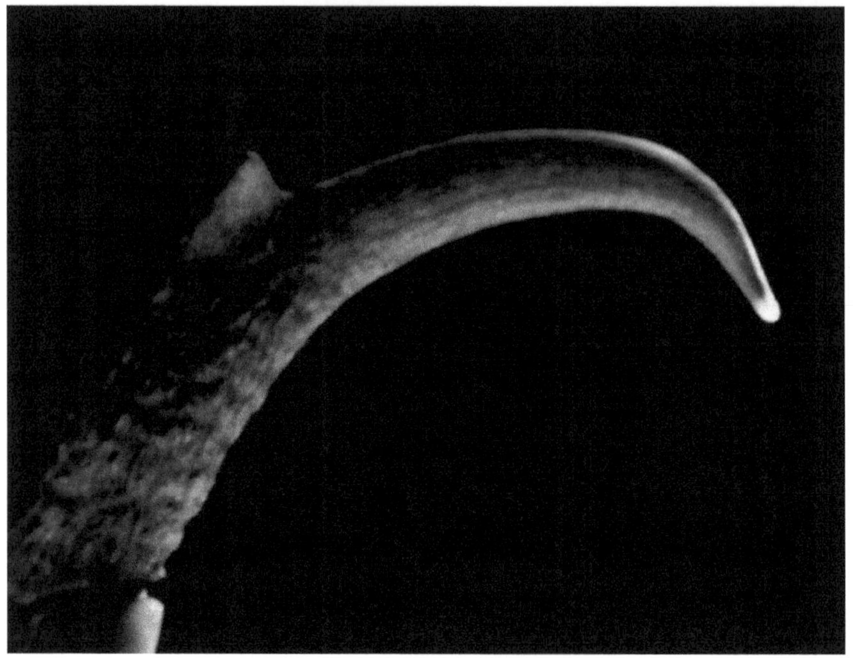

Figure 54. Horn with a "Lit" Tip
When held up to light, the tip lights up.

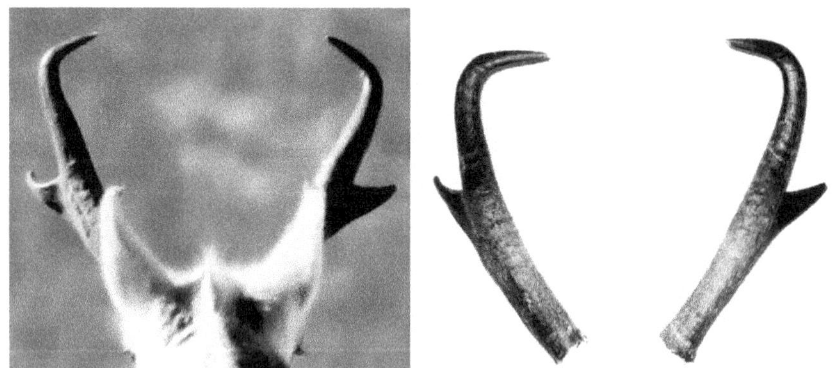

"Are those my horns I lost last year?" Horns not found and still somewhere in the wild (left), and horns I found and are in my 2021 collection (right).

Figure 55. Keeping Horns Display Ready
No, I don't really use my dishwasher!

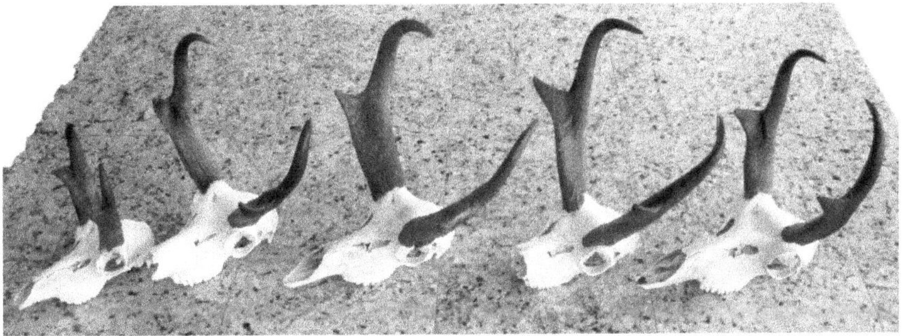

Figure 56. Horn Display of Five Matching Sets of Horns
These are not hunting trophies, each horn I found individually.

Figure 57. Keep Your Eye on the Horn!
While observing the herd of 20 pronghorn, I noticed four buck totaling eight horns; two of those horns are already missing. Can you tell which ones?

Those would be the most likely areas to find a horn. While fence crossings and frequented trails are the most likely areas to find a horn, finding a horn may take days and feel like it is looking for a needle in a haystack. I consider finding a horn as a gift from God, as He delights me while spending time alone with Him in the vast wilderness. Over time with persistence, horns are found. I found one horn at a coyote's den site where sadly the coyote had perished during recent arctic cold snap. Each horn is unique and is an artifact of a whole year which represents ten percent of that pronghorn's life. Fun and rewarding! Here are some pictures just for horn spotting practice, Figures 58-59. Can you spot the horn?

Figure 58. Spot the Horns - 1

Figure 59. Spot the Horns - 2

Here is a humorous anecdote to help remember that pronghorn horns are hollow. True story: I brought four of my favorite horns to some cohorts for a show-n-tell luncheon. The team was very impressed. One member chuckled and tongue-in-cheek proclaimed these horns are the perfect metaphor for management. "Like management," he said, "pronghorn horns are unique, impressive looking, have more than one good point, and can even appear threatening. But upon closer inspection, it becomes apparent that they are hollow on the inside." The group burst out in laughter!

My favorite pronghorn ever during all of my pronghorn-safari adventures is shown in Figure 60. I call him, ***The One***. I met him one-on-one in a field on June 2021, and later in the season with his sleek summer fur in September, shown way back in Figure 6. This fearless pronghorn allowed me to take some very close photos. What a treasured opportunity!

Figure 60. Pronghorn Buck Proudly Displays His Horns

In a rare one-on-one encounter, this pronghorn buck was proud to walk back and forth coming as close as 100 yards, while I took pictures. I named him, "The One." Quite a show off, but it was a very memorable encounter with nature. Perhaps he was curious when he saw the flash from my camera.

*"Impressive prong—
you win!"*

{ 11 }

The Adventure Continues

The call of opportunity launched me into this eighteen-month pronghorn field research project. It has been an amazing experience with many unanticipated discoveries and has really changed my perspective on the importance of wildlife conservation. The pronghorn species is a patchwork of herd communities who live life happily (or sometimes not) among themselves and who merge and disperse with other herds of pronghorn which total over 1 million individual animals across North America. The merging of herds is particularly striking in areas where they migrate in the winter and spring every year, such as the Wyoming areas near Grand Teton and Sublette County. As habitat is encroached upon by human development, the pronghorn retreat accordingly.

Within this literary work, I presented my technical findings and shared photographs I took in exploring pronghorn in their natural habitat while describing the events and surprises along the way. Aside from their beauty, speed, and iconic embodiment as a symbol of the American West, my first impression of pronghorn was their remarkable curiosity and fearlessness. In the field, they would approach me and stare me down. To be detected almost immediately in the field is a testimony to the pronghorn's keen eyesight, hearing, and smell. Their sight is magnified eight times with a movement-detection range of four miles. Pronghorn are social and often move as a herd when faced with a predator. Pronghorn can be seen lying in the field chewing their cud, ruminating, but most often they are in motion walking and grazing on choice blades of grass and succulent forbs. Pronghorn males often mark their territory and trail junctures by scraping the ground with their front hoof and depositing excrement on the spot in a SPUD ritual. Pronghorn love to gather and run, sometimes slipping by quietly behind my back only 200-300 yards away at nearly full speed – they can seem to mysteriously appear or disappear. Pronghorn will often graze just out of view across the prairie, behind a rolling hill with only one or two males perched in a prominent look-out position. The annual pronghorn cycle involves rutting and mating in September, horns falling off in late November, and fawns birthing in May. One of my favorite motivators in getting out there on the prairie is the hope of finding a horn – difficult as finding a needle in a haystack, yet unparalleled in excitement. Despite the daunting challenge, I have amassed a collection of 56 horns in a short eighteen month research period. Yes, pronghorn are quite amazing creatures, and the wilderness environment – endless grasslands and prairie – evokes feelings of insignificance, timelessness, loneliness, offset with God's loving presence stamped with His infinite power and abundance. The experience gives rise to the realization that we live in great uncertainty and are helpless individual humans. Even as the most special of God's creations, we have only fleeting time here on Earth.

You do not even know what will happen tomorrow!
What is your life? You are a mist that appears for a
little while and then vanishes. ***James 4:14***

I have often thought of continuing field research with pronghorn and other wildlife by enlisting with Colorado Parks & Wildlife (CPW). In a random coincidence, I happened to drive right past the Colorado Springs CPW office. Hiking buddy, Dave, and I were driving to the Templeton-Gap hiking trailhead when we drove right past CPW office. "That's where I would inquire," I mused. That could be a viable option when transitioning into retirement in the future. This pronghorn field research has left a lasting impact on my life – what will the future hold for pronghorn adventures and me... And someday soon, maybe you?

Another trophy from a majestic pronghorn, recently found and added to my collection.

As territory shrinks due to ceaseless construction and urban sprawl, king pronghorn wonders, "Gee, patrols around here keep getting shorter. Is it time for new pastures?"

As territory shrinks due to ceaseless construction and urban sprawl, king pronghorn wonders, "Gee, patrols around here keep getting shorter. Is it time for new pastures?"

Epilogue

This 18 month pronghorn field research adventure has been a personally enriching opportunity for me in many ways. Lingering emotions I have encountered after every safari and into the present continue to be the feeling of a fading-away pronghorn world, as depicted in the impressionist photograph in Figure 61. Pronghorn horn and skull artifacts such as in Figure 62 will fade away as new residential areas replace open prairie where these things could be found. The bulldozers keep coming to repurpose eons-old land once home to our resident pronghorn community, Figures 63-65. The herd will retreat to adjacent expansive grasslands further away from human development and will remain unchanged for years to come. It is with mild despondency, I have witnessed this particular yet often unnoticed pronghorn family diminish from fifty-five, to twenty, and very soon zero.

Figure 61. Pronghorn Special Effect Photograph
Picture taken at dusk, a buck gazes across his land, in slow retreat from man.

Figure 62. Pronghorn Horns on Skull

Figure 63. Pronghorn Thrive on the Edge of Human Development

Figure 64. Bulldozers Forever Change the Pronghorn Landscape

Figure 65. Gazing at Bulldozers, His Grassland Will Soon Be Gone

Addendum on Left Hook

I continued to observe the neighborhood herd over the summer, now numbering 25 pronghorn. In August, I discovered a unique pronghorn. On page 27, I introduced a pronghorn I named "Left Hook" due to the freakish downward-pointed prong of his left horn.

Left Hook must have won a joust and scored his own harem, and he is now surrounded with female companionship going into mating season. Well done, Lefty!

Pronghorn horns are unique in size and shape, but this was a marked distinction. I was initially saddened when I saw this apparent deformity as well as amazed at the uniqueness of the horn shape. I assumed Left Hook would be destined to be a roaming bachelor, living life as a social outcast from the herd. But he proved me wrong!

Left Hook has overcome "looking different" and transformed it into a superpower! What is your superpower?

And so it goes, Left Hook must have won a joust and scored his own harem. What's more, Left Hook has overcome "looking different" and transformed it into a superpower! Not knowing the details of what happens in the prairie wilds of Colorado, the end result is that Left Hook is now surrounded with female companionship going into mating season. Well done, Lefty!

And as an addendum on Professor Jim... He has gone on to serve with Colorado Parks & Wildlife (CPW) meeting many giving, passionate wildlife enthusiasts and has participated in ten CPW activities by year end, 2022. CPW is all about serving the community to preserve wildlife for generations of enjoyment by all. By taking care of wildlife, the way is paved for all to know God and share in His gift of the wild outdoors. Enjoying wildlife is all about "getting out there" and observing — soaking in the beauty all around!

Let me leave you with words from my CPW cohort, Jaimie, who inspires with a profound description of her Colorado experience:

Today commemorates one year in this amazing state of Colorado. I've had amazing times and good memories. I regret nothing. God has truly put me where I belong and given me the best people, best food, best sites, and most amazing wildlife. I encourage all of you to quit pursuing what the world expects and pursue your dreams. What do you want to get out of life? I know my goals are to explore, meet interesting people, laugh a LOT, grow as a person, help others grow, and love everyone. It's a simple answer for me. I am doing what I'm made to do, and that is spread joy, peace, and love and bring recognition of the beauty that can be revealed if you just take your time and open your eyes... Just do it! You only live once (YOLO)

— Jaimie Sommerfeld, 2022

Left Hook ruminating, a quiet, meditative display of self confidence and joy of being one with Nature. An example for us all.

References

1. Alsheimer, C. (2017, 1Sep). "The Science Behind Antler Growing and Velvet Shedding." Retrieved from https://www.realtree.com/deer-hunting/galleries/the-science-behind-antler-growing-and-velvet-shedding
Figure retrieved from https://www.realtree.com/sites/default/files/styles/x_base_767/public/content/essays/realtree-velvet-shed-alsheimer00003490dsc6468.jpg?itok=BeMEo4EN
2. American Southwest, (2022). "Nine Mile Canyon (Pronghorn Petroglyph)." Retrieved from https://www.americansouthwest.net/utah/nine-mile-canyon/index.html
3. AMNH, (2022). "Prehistoric Pronghorn: Ancient Antelope." Retrieved from https://www.arizonamuseumofnaturalhistory.org/explore-the-museum/exhibitions/previous-exhibitions/prehistoric-pronghorn-ancient-antelope
4. Animal Spot, (2022, 2Jan). "Animal Spot: Pronghorn." Retrieved from https://www.animalspot.net/pronghorn.html
5. Big Sky Stories, Pronghorns, (2021). "Big Sky Stories, Pronghorns." Retrieved from https://www.visitbigsky.com/get-inspired/big-sky-stories/interesting-facts-about-pronghorns-1
6. Boxerville, (2020). "Pronghorn sound when its warning you to stay away video." Retrieved from https://youtu.be/y6_KxG_xFM4
7. Byers, J., (2003). "Built for Speed: A Year in the Life of Pronghorn." Harvard University Press; Cambridge MA (ISBN 0674011422)
8. Car Speaker Land, (2018, 8Jul). "What Does Deer Poop Look Like? Deer Poop Matters!" Retrieved from https://medium.com/@car-

speakerland/what-does-deer-poop-look-like-deer-poop-matters-a3f65cdd9056
9. CDC, (2021, Dec). "Mortality in the United States, 2020." Retrieved from https://www.cdc.gov/nchs/products/databriefs/db427.htm
10. ColoradoOutdoorsMag, (2011). "The Pronghorn Rut in Colorado video." Retrieved from https://youtu.be/tSVu5Kp5HOg
11. Crause, B., (2017, 26Jun). "How Can the Pronghorn Cross the Fence?" Retrieved from https://blog.nature.org/science/2017/06/26/how-pronghorn-cross-fence-wildlife-connectivity/
12. Delorenzo, J., (2018, 20Mar). "Beginner's Guide to Shed Hunting." Retrieved from https://gearjunkie.com/outdoor/hunt-fish/how-to-shed-hunt
13. Geology.com, (2022). "Petroglyph," Retrieved from https://geology.com/articles/petroglyphs.shtml
14. Go Hunt, (2014, 20Aug). "Wildlife fences - friend or foe to big game?" Retrieved from https://www.gohunt.com/read/wildlife-fences-friend-or-foe-to-big-game#gs.ls0s1n
15. Guthrie, W. & Ferguson, J.,(1815). "A New Geographical, Historical, and Commercial Grammar and Present State of the Several Kingdoms of the World." Vol. 2. Philadelphia, USA: Johnson & Warner. p. 308.
16. Hall, B. K., (2005). "Horns and Ossicones." Retrieved from https://www.sciencedirect.com/topics/biochemistry-genetics-and-molecular-biology/antelope
17. Harris, C., (2014). "A Symbolic State: Home on the Range". Kansas! Magazine. 2014 (Spring): 17–26, page 19.
18. Huffman, B. (2022). "An Ultimate Ungulate Fact Sheet." Retrieved from http://www.ultimateungulate.com/Artiodactyla/Antilocapra_americana.html
19. Humphrey, R., Kayser, M. and Meyer. J. (2018, 1Mar). "Shed Hunting 101." Retrieved from https://www.mossyoak.com/our-obsession/blogs/how-to/shed-hunting-101
20. Jessica, (2013, 28Mar). "Bromo-Seltzer, Emerson Drug Co. Baltimore, MD." Retrieved from https://oldmainartifacts.wordpress.com/

2013/03/28/bromo-seltzer-emerson-drug-co-baltimore-md/
21. Kmcandre, (2014, 18Sep). “Pronghorn Introduction.” Retrieved from https://kmcandre.wordpress.com/2014/09/18/pronghorn-introduction/
21a. Lagos, A. (2022). “advertisement for Animal Horns.”Retrieved from https://www.exportersindia.com/lucky-omo-concept/animal-horns-2739117.htm
22. Lomax, J. A., (1910). "A Home on The Range". Cowboy Songs and Other Frontier Ballads. New York: Sturgis & Walton Company. pp. 39–43. LCCN 10030589. OCLC 7288334.
23. MFWP, (2022a). “Conservation; Wildlife Management; Pronghorn (Antelope).” Retrieved from https://fwp.mt.gov/conservation/wildlife-management/antelope
24. MFWP, (2022b). “Field Guide for Pronghorn.” Retrieved from https://fieldguide.mt.gov/speciesDetail.aspx?elcode=AMALD01010
25. MFWP, (2022c). “How to Build Fence with Wildlife in Mind.” Retrieved from https://www.nrcs.usda.gov/Internet/FSE_DOCUMENTS/nrcs142p2_026389.pdf
26. Miller, B., (2017, 21Apr). “Are Pronghorn Millions of Years Old?” Retrieved from https://www.grandviewoutdoors.com/lifestyle/pronghorns-millions-years-old
27. Montana Outdoors, (2013, 23Sep). “Elk, Deer and Antelope Hunting.” Retrieved from https://www.montanaoutdoor.com/2013/09/elk-deer-and-antelope-hunting-forecast-by-fwp/
28. National Geographic, (2022). “Pronghorn.” Retrieved from https://www.nationalgeographic.com/animals/mammals/facts/pronghorn
29. Nature Works, (2022). “Pronghorn - Antilocapra Americana.” Retrieved from https://nhpbs.org/natureworks/pronghorn.htm
29a. Newberry, G (2022). “Pronghorn Phylogeny.” Retrieved from https://gretchennewberry.wordpress.com/2017/03/07/pronghorns-and-phylogeny/
30. NPS-Bryce, (2022). “Bryce Canyon NP, Pronghorn.” Retrieved from

https://www.nps.gov/brca/planyourvisit/upload/pronghorn.pdf
31. NPS-Lewis, (2022). "Lewis & Clark National Historic Trail, Pronghorn." Retrieved from https://www.nps.gov/articles/pronghorn.htm
32. NPS-Tule, (2022). "Prehistoric Life of Tule Springs; Tule Springs Pronghorn; Tule Springs Fossil Beds National Monument." Retrieved from https://www.nps.gov/articles/000/tule-springs-pronghorn.htm
33. Pesaturo, J. (2019, 14Mar). "Pronghorn Tracks and Sign." Retrieved from https://winterberrywildlife.ouroneacrefarm.com/2019/03/14/pronghorn-tracks-and-sign/
SPUD link: https://youtu.be/x29HQwYR5fI
34. Popescu, A., (2017, 16Apr). "America's pronghorns are survivors of a mass extinction." Retrieved from https://m.theindependentbd.com/arcprint/details/90196/2017-04-16
35. Rovira, M. Q., (2017, 15Jan). "It's a Matter of Horns," Retrieved from https://allyouneedisbiology.wordpress.com/2017/01/15/mammals-horns-antlers/
36. San Diego Zoo, (2022). "Pronghorn." Retrieved from https://animals.sandiegozoo.org/animals/pronghorn
37. Stewart, M., (2020, 19Jun). "Pronghorn are safe: Wildlife not trapped, in danger due to northern El Paso County development, says CPW." Retrieved from https://gazette.com/thetribune/pronghorn-are-safe-wildlife-not-trapped-in-danger-due-to-northern-el-paso-county-development/article_eb74760a-e838-11e8-bdbf-031c594d2d84.html
38. Tetrapod, (2022). "Release the Fossil Pronghorns!!" Retrieved from https://tetzoo.com/blog/2021/11/22/release-the-fossil-pronghorns
39. Treehugger, (2020, 21May). "Nature Blows My Mind! North America's Fastest Land Animal Can Outrun a Cheetah." Retrieved from https://www.treehugger.com/nature-blows-mind-north-americas-fastest-land-animal-can-outrun-cheetah-4858539
40. Urbigkit, C.and Gocke, M., (2010). "Path of the Pronghorn." Boyds Mills Press, Inc.; Honesdale PA (ISBN 978-1-59078-756-4)
41. Wikipedia, (2022), "Pronghorn." Retrieved from https://en.wikipedia.org/wiki/Pronghorn

42. Wildlife Conservation Society, (2018, 15Aug). "Study of greater Yellowstone pronghorn finds highway crossing structures a conservation success." Retrieved from https://phys.org/news/2018-08-greater-yellowstone-pronghorn-highway-success.html

43. Yule, J., (2019, 28Sep). "Pronghorn The Challenge video." Retrieved from https://www.youtube.com/watch?v=5nU3o4Tie5E

Glossary

Acronym/Term	Meaning
AFB	Air Force Base
antelope	swift-running deer like ruminant with smooth hair and upward-pointing horns of a group native to Africa and Asia that includes the gazelles, impala, gnus, and elands
antler	each of the branched horns on the head of adult male deer family, are made of bone, and are grown and cast annually.
bovid	mammal of the cattle family, bovidae, which comprises the biological family of cloven-hoofed, ruminant mammals that includes cattle, deer, pronghorn, sheep, goats, etc.
buck	male pronghorn antelope
CPW	Colorado Parks & Wildlife
cud	regurgitated, partly-digested food comprised of plants
doe	female pronghorn antelope
fawn	baby pronghorn antelope

forbs	forb or phorb is an herbaceous flowering plant that is not a graminoid (grass, sedge, or rush). The term "forb" may be used for subdividing popular guides to wildflowers, distinguishing them from other categories such as grasses, sedges, shrubs, and trees. Some examples of forbs are clovers, sunflowers, daylilies, and milkweed
fork	point where something, especially a road or river, divides into two parts
hackle	erectile hairs along the back of a dog or other animal that rise when it is angry or alarmed
herd	group of pronghorn antelope
horn	hard permanent outgrowth, often curved and pointed, found in pairs on the heads of cattle, sheep, goats, giraffes, etc. and consisting of a core of bone encased in keratinized skin.
jackalope	mythical animal of North American folklore described as a jackrabbit with antelope horns
keratin	fibrous protein forming the main structural constituent of hair, feathers, hoofs, claws, and horns
MFWP	Montana Fish, Wildlife & Parks
mental search image	Also known as a mind picture, is a mental skill used to find partially hidden objects in the surrounding environment
petroglyph	rock carving, especially a prehistoric one

prong	each of two or more pointed parts at the end of a fork
pronghorn	deer like North American mammal with a stocky body, long slim legs, and black horns that are shed and regrown annually
phylogeny	In biology, phylogeny or phylogenetics is the study of the evolutionary history and relationships among groups of organisms. These relationships are determined by phylogenetic inference methods that focus on observed heritable traits, such as DNA sequences, protein amino acid sequences, or morphology
ruminant	mammal of suborder Ruminantia which includes six different cud-chewing families: Tragulidae, Giraffidae, Antilocapridae, Moschidae, Cervidae, and Bovidae
ruminate	a. to chew over again. Chew cud, as in when bovid animals such as cows or sheep chew the cud, they slowly chew their regurgitated, partly-digested food over and over again in their mouth before finally swallowing it. Bovids have four-chambered stomachs b. think deeply about something.
rut	during the rut (known as the rutting period), males often rub their horns on trees or shrubs, fight with each other, and herd estrus females together. These displays make the male conspicuous and aids in mate selection.

safari	expedition to observe or hunt animals in their natural habitat
scat	also known as excrement, poop, feces, or stool, is the universal metabolic byproduct of the digestive tract
SPUD	Sniff-Paw-Urinate-Defecate
steppe	semi-desert grassland
ungulate	family of hoofed animals
URL	Uniform Resource Locator (or Internet web address)
USAF	United States Air Force
zooarchaeology	study of animal artifacts

Book Format Options

Estimated Retail Price (USD)	Description
$ 49.95	Heirloom 7x10 color Hardback
$ 39.95	Premium 7x10 color Paperback
$19.95	Price-Concious Value format, 6x9 B&W Paperback
--	eBOOK and Audiobook also available

Heirloom 7x10" Hardback

Premium 7x10" Paperback

6x9" Black & White Paperback

Kindle, or Audiobook

Discounts available on bulk print format orders
james.szczur07@gmail.com

Additional Reviewers Comments

What reviewers have said about, *Exploring the Neighborhood Pronghorn Community (2nd edition)*:

Award winning author and wildlife enthusiast Professor Jim Szczur explores pronghorn near his Colorado home. He draws upon his own encounters with pronghorn and presents photographs he took during the experience to tell his story. He explains how this iconic animal of the American West evolved and adapted for survival since before the Ice Age. He then focuses on pronghorn activity today and in his own neighborhood where herd members work in tandem to defend fawns and ward off potential predators, such as coyotes, as well as the animals' use of vocalizations and musk deposits to signal danger or delineate territorial boundaries. He touches on other wildlife and artifacts present in the local pronghorn habitat and expounds on the sport and joy of horn hunting. Szczur's passion for pronghorn is heartfelt and admirable, as he brings a fresh perspective and photographically enhanced tribute to his local pronghorn herd.

Dave Fromme (Colorado Springs resident and avid reader): The book captured my curiosity, evoking many questions about the pronghorn. I realized there was a lot I did not know. The pictures are amazing — they actualized the experience and continued to hold my attention as the author unveiled the science with the story. I was amazed at all the scientific facts about the pronghorn, very organized and well referenced. Each chapter presented a different point of view and enriched my understanding about the pronghorn. The horn hunting anecdotes were superb, and the conclusion summarized the pronghorn adventure and left me feeling a little sad that I had missed the actual experience. I learned a lot and had a feeling of shared experience with Professor Jim in the wilderness. Thank you for a great read!

Christine FIVE-STAR rating (Goodreads renowned reviewer (ave rating 3.7) with over 500 reviews, 18 May 2023):

I was able to read this book because it was gifted to my husband from the author who happens to be a coworker. As a new Coloradan, I've enjoyed reading about history & urban legends, so I welcomed the chance to learn about one aspect of the nature of the state. And because we reside in a town in the plains region of Colorado, I've had numerous opportunities to observe herds of pronghorn. As a born and raised Californian, I was instantly struck by the animal as they looked like African antelope, and I had no idea we had animals like this in the United States. I was literally today, reading this book, when it occurred to me that "where the deer and the antelope play" line of *Home on the Range* was referring to these animals. I had been wanting to investigate them more and then this book fell into my lap!

I truly enjoyed reading this. I'd never been able to observe these antelope up close, because I was usually driving and they would be far out in a field. **The pictures were fantastic** — I'd never realized how unique their horns were, and I love the texture/colors of their coats. **They're adorable! The poofy white booties** (which have a purpose as I also learned in the book)! **The author's writing voice is humorous and approachable for any reader. I learned so much about these animals and was frankly amazed** by some of the facts (see cheetah comparison).

Probably the most depressing thing is the destruction of the pronghorn habitat. Many Coloradans bemoan the urban sprawl that is encroaching on all animals' once vast home. No one is more concerned than my husband and I about this, as Colorado's wild, natural beauty was what drew us to moving here. California had become a concrete jungle of trash, graffiti, and high-density housing; Colorado seemed a utopia of being more one with the land. **I admire Professor Jim being able to spend hours amongst these beautiful animals in their natural habitat in the noble pursuit of spreading awareness about the antelope** during a time when some of us in other parts of the country weren't even allowed outside [due to COVID restrictions]. There is nothing more important than preserving the land as it has been for centuries instead of permanently destroying it for another Starbucks or dental office. **Seeing my local pronghorn herd brings me far more joy and peace, and I will be very sad when/if the day comes that they have been pushed so far outside of my community that this is no longer an everyday sight.**

https://www.goodreads.com/book/show/123075808-exploring-the-neighborhood-pronghorn-community

Award Winning Author

Book Award

7 Most SURPRISING Reads of 2022

December 29, 2022

You know that feeling you get when you walk into a seemingly dark, deserted room and everybody and their dog jumps out and hollers, "SURPRISE!!"? It's so unexpected and sudden. You may feel astonished. Happy. Giddy. In shock. Or the surprise may give you a heart attack.

Well. We came across some reads this year that surprised us. (The good kind of surprise, not the heart attack kind.) The books below are all by authors that are new to us. That we never heard of before grabbing their book and deciding to take "a shot in the dark." All feature:

- **Excellent writing that's briskly paced**
- **Strong, sturdy characterizations**
- **A solid plot that's unusually clever, creative, fresh, and/or informative**
- **A transcendent theme or message**
- **Are page turners worth re-reading**

These titles include indie and/or first-time authors. Several are either self-published or published by small imprints. **And they're all surprisingly GOOD. Engaging. Interesting.** Quick as Kimber after a bowl of kibble. Or extra crispy bacon.

Most have had little to no exposure. And that's too bad. Because these are all worthwhile reads. Think "breath of fresh bookish air." *Yeah, baby!*

So… drum roll please for the 7 **Most Surprising Reads of 2022** (in no particular order):

1. The Silver Gate, By Kristin Bailey (2017)

2. The Chronicles of the Imaginarium Geographica: Here, There Be Dragons, by James A. Owen (2006)

3. The Lawyer's Angel, By Scott Allen Benkie (2022)

4. The Legend of Lilia, By Christopher P. Redwine (2022)

5. Exploring the Neighborhood Pronghorn Community (Second Edition), By James Szczur (2022)

6. When the Day Comes, By Gabrielle Meyer (2022)

7. Echoes in the Stars, By Gordon Frisbie (2022)

Pages & Paws

Writing, Reading, and Rural Life With a Border Collie

https://pagesandpaws.com/2022/12/29/7-most-surprising-reads-of-2022/

Lessons Learned Class Presentation

Lessons from

EXPLORING THE NEIGHBORHOOD PRONGHORN COMMUNITY

Second Edition

BY JAMES SZCZUR

JamesSzczur.wordpress.com

Book Lessons

- The pronghorn is a wonder of Nature
- Pronghorn vs. Antelope
- Most Similar Animal?
- Pronghorn Behavior
- Technical inaccuracies "out there"
- Horn Hunting is Fun!
- Conservation and Urban Sprawl
- Conclusion
- Reviewers Comments
- References

The Pronghorn is a wonder of Nature

(photo credit: Alison Hardenburgh, Northern Desert Photography)

Similar to deer and the African antelope families, but the pronghorn is a unique species native to North America and is the only animal that has branched horns and sheds them annually.

Pronghorn vs. Antelope

- Similar in appearance
- Pronghorn Uniqueness:
  - Different horns
  - Lives in North America
  - Only one species

Most Similar Animal?

- DNA analysis determined pronghorn and giraffe are closest relatives
- The pronghorn is a "sports car" version of the deer
  - Faster
  - Lighter bones
  - Sheds antlers/horns
  - Skulls similar shape & size

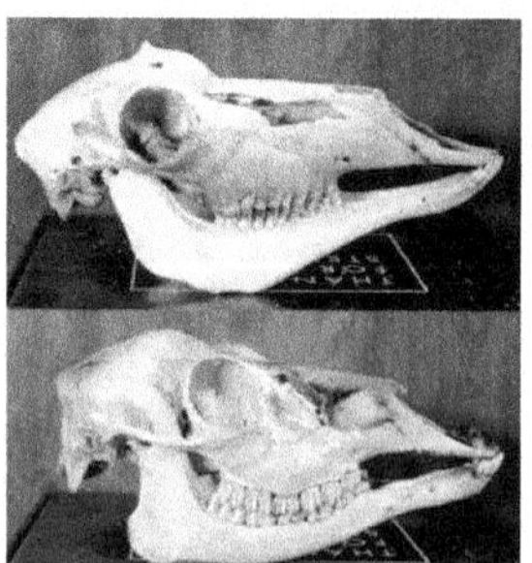

Left:

Pronghorn (top)

Mule deer (bottom, with heavier bone and square jaw)

Although the pronghorn is the smaller animal, they have larger eyes, roughly equal skulls, and significantly lighter bone compared to the mule deer.

Pronghorn Behavior

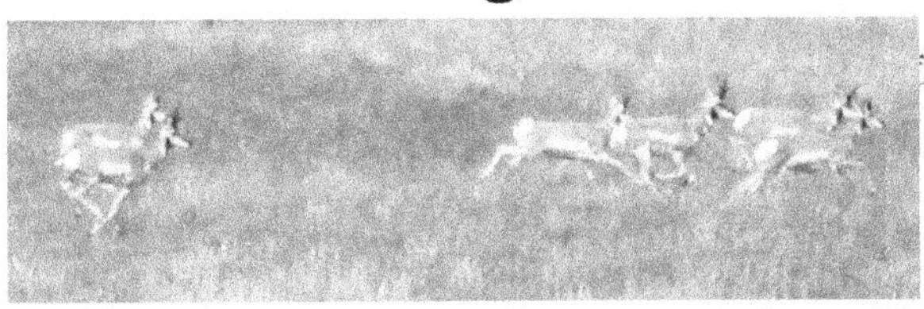

- Curious and not afraid
  Confident in their speed
- Territorial and social
- Rutting, like deer and defend harem

Technical inaccuracies "out there"

Eye size equal to horse or African elephant?

"With eyes as large as those of elephants" "They have the same eye size as African elephants"
"Pronghorn eyes are the same size as horse eyes and are nearly as large as elephant eyes"

Measured eye socket	Animal
38 mm	Mule Deer
43 mm	Pronghorn
55 mm	Horse

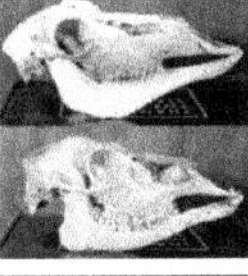

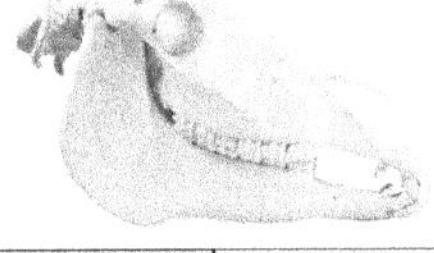

- ✓ Chart measurements were taken by Professor Jim at his Colorado Springs laboratory.
- ✓ Skull eye socket gives easily measurable relative eye size, but of course are larger than eye size because they account for the eye plus connective and muscle tissue.

Same eye size as a horse?

FALSE

Reported Eyeball Diameter	Animal
42 mm	Horse
30 mm	Reindeer
30 mm	Asian Elephant
40 mm	African Elephant
36 mm	Pronghorn
25 mm	Human
50 mm	Ostrich
40 mm	Camel
37 mm	East African oryx antelope 170 lbs

- Chart data form Howland, *et. al.*
- Asian elephant's eye is 20% smaller than the pronghorn.
- African elephant's eye much larger than Asian, 33% larger.
- But the comparison breaks down miserably, as elephants are know for relatively small eyes and poor eyesight.
- Other reported eye sizes listed are for comparison.

Same size eyes as African elephant?

FALSE

Technical inaccuracies "out there"

Prong forms by pronged bone structure (false)

"bucks have prong-shaped bony horns that are covered by horn sheaths"

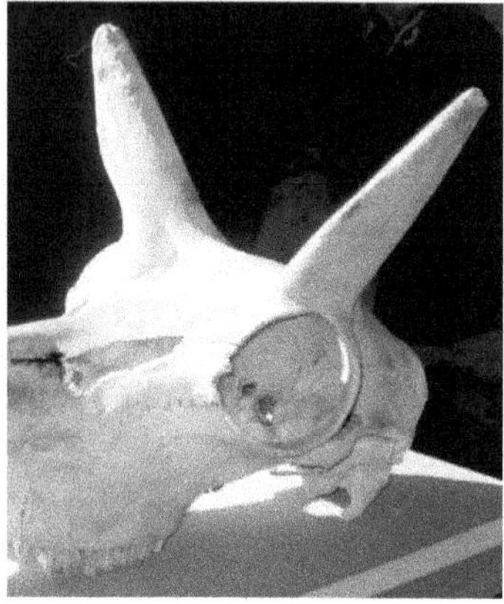

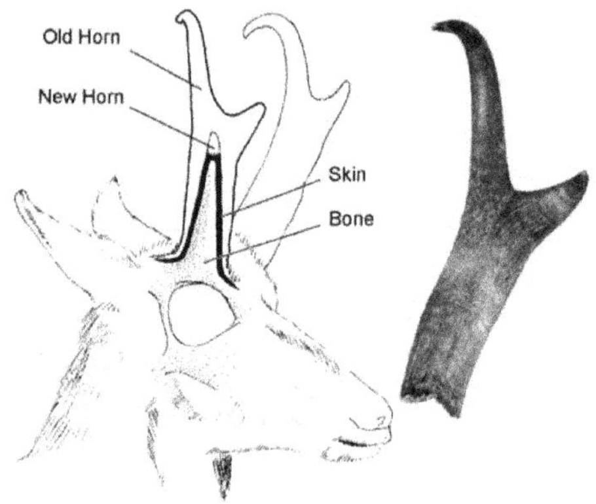

FALSE, the bone has no prong, but the horn does have a prong

Technical inaccuracies "out there"

Male and female grow horns equally (false)

"Pronghorn derive their names from short horns that both males and females grow"
"Both sexes carry these horns that are shed each year"

Harem of 4-5 does. (more, 10-12 "family")

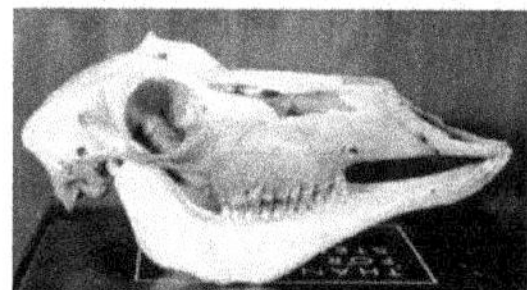

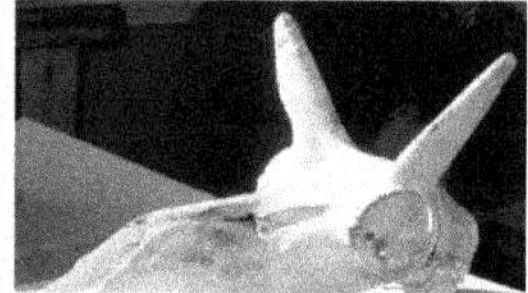

FALSE, female skulls do not have the horn-growing bone structure

FALSE, in Colorado Springs CO, harems number 10-12.

Technical inaccuracies "out there"

Male pronghorn horns grow near-vertically

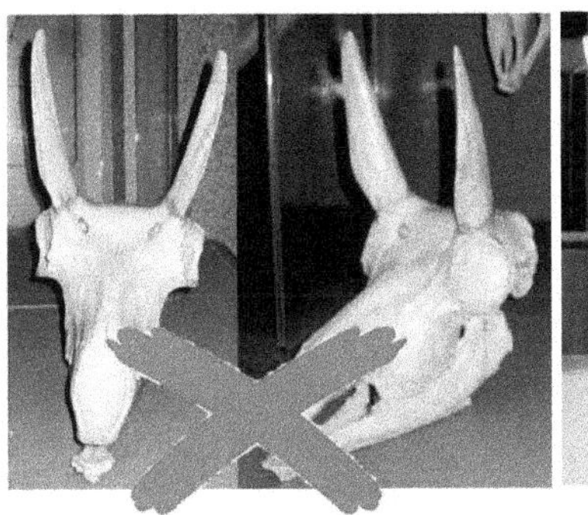

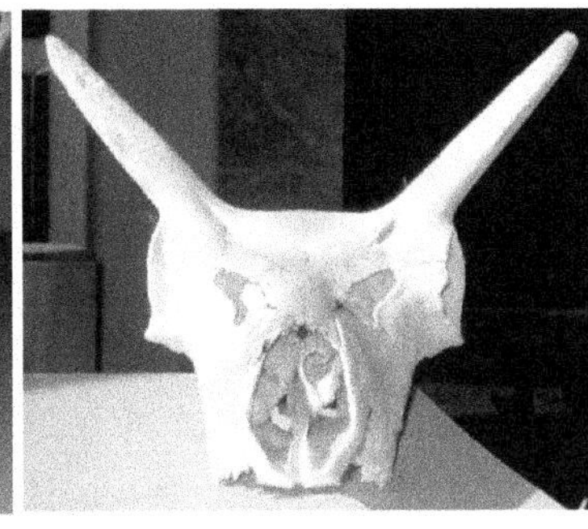

The pronghorn horn-bone structures project vertically and about 45-degrees outwardly from the top of each eye socket.

Technical inaccuracies "out there"

Pronghorn do not jump over fences (false)

FALSE, they can jump especially if startled, but both pronghorn and deer prefer to go under wire fence, as it is easier and less dangerous.

Technical inaccuracies "out there"

"Coyotes hunt in packs"
Hmm, what do you think? (research is fun!)

Coyotes are very social animals, **they do not form packs** but rather live in family groups. They will usually travel and hunt alone but sometimes join in loose pairs to take down prey.

U.S. National Park Service (NPS) https://www.nps.gov/articles/000/coyote-info.htm

Horn Hunting is Fun!

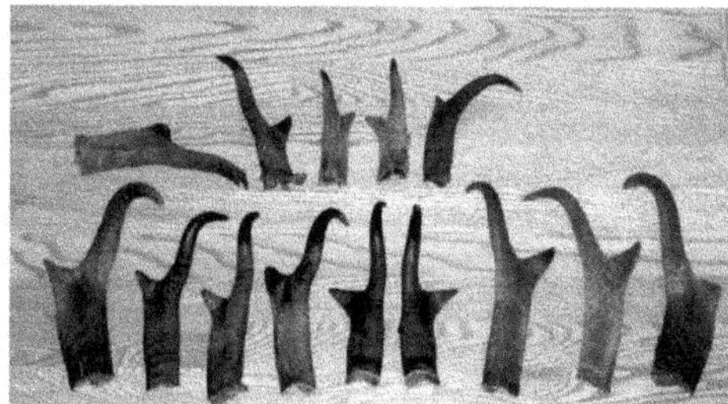

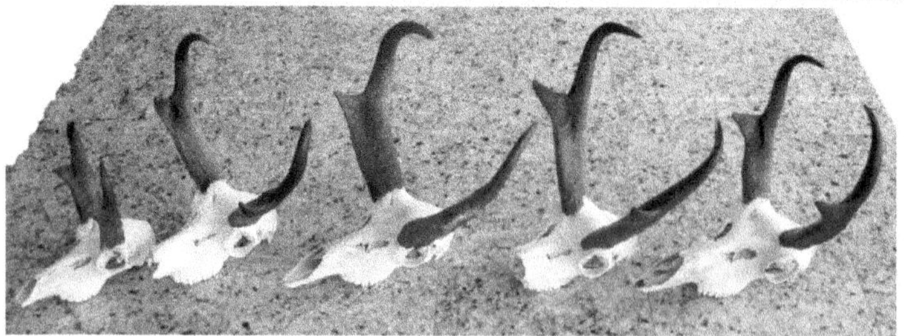

Conservation and Urban Sprawl

Pronghorn conservation is a success story, but the bulldozers of urban development push pronghorn further away.

Conclusion

The pronghorn is a wonder of Nature, its own unique species and most similar to deer. Pronghorn are very visible if you live in the Rocky Mountains plains area.

Contact your local wildlife or Nature center for further information on how to observe pronghorn where you live.

References

- Go Hunt, (2014, 20Aug). "Wildlife fences - friend or foe to big game?" Retrieved from https://www.gohunt.com/read/wildlife-fences-friend-or-foe-to-big-game#gs.lsOs1n
- Hardenburgh, Alison; Northern Desert Photography, northerndesertphotography.com/2021/09/12/pronghorn
- Howland, Merola, Basarab, "The allometry and scaling of the size of vertebrate eyes." Retrieved from www.sciencedirect.com/science/article/pii/S0042698904001646
- Huffman, B. (2022). "An Ultimate Ungulate Fact Sheet." Retrieved from http://www.ultimateungulate.com/Artiodactyla/Antilocapra_americana.html
- Kemp, A.D., (2014). "Eye Size and Visual Acuity Influence Vestibular Anatomy in Mammals." Retrieved from anatomypubs.onlinelibrary.wiley.com/doi/10.1002/ar.22892
- O'Gara BW, Matson G. 1975. Growth and casting of horns by pronghorns and exfoliation of horns by bovids. Journal of Mammalogy 56: 829–846
- Szczur, J., (2022). "Exploring the Neighborhood Pronghorn Community (second edition); Pronghorn Antelope Observation and Zooarchaeology in Colorado." Professor Jim Publishing, Inc, Colorado Springs, Colorado
- Wyoming Department of Transportation www.conteches.com/knowledge-center/case-studies/details/slug/wydot-highway-191---trappers-point

Pronghorn Doe (photo credit Jasmine Szczur)

www.ingramcontent.com/pod-product-compliance
Ingram Content Group UK Ltd.
Pitfield, Milton Keynes, MK11 3LW, UK
UKHW020140250726
13967UKWH00002B/779